THE COLLECTED COURSES OF
THE ACADEMY OF EUROPEAN LAW

Volume XXX/2

Legal Mobilization for Human Rights

THE COLLECTED COURSES OF THE ACADEMY OF EUROPEAN LAW

Edited by: Professor Neha Jain, Professor Claire Kilpatrick, Professor Sarah Nouwen, and Professor Joanne Scott

Assistant Editor: Joyce Davies

The Academy of European Law is housed at the European University Institute in Florence, Italy. The Academy holds annual advanced-level summer courses focusing on topical, cutting-edge issues in human rights law and the law of the European Union. The courses are taught by highly qualified scholars and practitioners in a highly interactive environment. General courses involve the examination of the field as a whole through a particular thematic, conceptual, or philosophical lens or look at a theme in the context of the overall body of law. Specialized courses bring together a number of speakers exploring a specific theme in depth. Together, they are published as monographs and edited volumes in the Collected Courses of the Academy of European Law series. The Collected Courses series has been published by Oxford University Press since 2000. The series contains publications on both foundational and pressing issues in human rights law and the law of the European Union.

OTHER TITLES IN THE SERIES INCLUDE:

The UK's Withdrawal from the EU
A Legal Analysis
Michael Dougan

Justifying Contract in Europe
Political Philosophies of European Contract Law
Martijn W. Hesselink

Contemporary Challenges to EU Legality
Edited by Claire Kilpatrick and Joanne Scott

Reframing Human Rights in a Turbulent Era
Gráinne de Búrca

New Legal Approaches to Studying the Court of Justice
Revisiting Law in Context
Edited by Claire Kilpatrick and Joanne Scott

EU Law Beyond EU Borders
The Extraterritorial Reach of EU Law
Edited by Marise Cremona and Joanne Scott

Freedom of Religion, Secularism, and Human Rights
Edited by Nehal Bhuta

EU Administrative Law
Third Edition
Paul Craig

Legal Mobilization for Human Rights

Edited by

GRÁINNE DE BÚRCA

OXFORD
UNIVERSITY PRESS

OXFORD
UNIVERSITY PRESS

Great Clarendon Street, Oxford, OX2 6DP,
United Kingdom

Oxford University Press is a department of the University of Oxford.
It furthers the University's objective of excellence in research, scholarship,
and education by publishing worldwide. Oxford is a registered trade mark of
Oxford University Press in the UK and in certain other countries

First Edition published in 2022

Published in the United States of America by Oxford University Press
198 Madison Avenue, New York, NY 10016, United States of America

British Library Cataloguing in Publication Data
Data available

Library of Congress Control Number: 2021951866

ISBN 978–0–19–286657–8

DOI: 10.1093/oso/9780192866578.001.0001

Printed and bound by
CPI Group (UK) Ltd, Croydon, CR0 4YY

Contents

Notes on Contributors

Carlos Andrés Baquero-Díaz holds an LLM in international legal studies from NYU Law, where he was a Hauser Global Scholar and 2019 recipient of the Jerome Lipper Award. He has a JD from Universidad de los Andes (Bogotá, Colombia), where he graduated *cum laude*, and a BA in political science from the same university. Currently, he is a JSD student at NYU Law working on issues related to property and environment law in the Brazilian Amazon region. His research interests focus on discrimination, participation, environment law, property, and climate change. He has worked at different research centres and NGOs such as NYU's Center for Human Rights and Global Justice, the Center for the Study of the Law, Justice and Society (Dejusticia), the Columbia Center for Sustainable Investment, and the Comunidad de Juristas Akubadaura.

Gráinne de Búrca is Florence Ellinwood Allen Professor of Law at NYU. She is Director of the Hauser Global Law School and Co-director of the Jean Monnet Center. Her fields of research include European Union law and human rights law. She is co-author with Paul Craig of the OUP textbook *EU Law*, currently in its seventh edition, and author of the book *Reframing Human Rights in a Turbulent Era* (2021). She is co-editor-in-chief of the *International Journal of Constitutional Law (I•CON)* and a Corresponding Fellow of the British Academy.

Christine Chinkin, FBA, CMG, previously Professor of International Law, is currently Professorial Research Fellow at the Centre for Women Peace and Security at LSE and Global Law Professor at the University of Michigan. She is co-author of *The Boundaries of International Law: A Feminist Analysis* (2000), *The Making of International Law* (2007), and *International Law and New Wars* (2017). She was a member of the Human Rights Advisory Panel in Kosovo for six years and Scientific Adviser to the Council of Europe's Committee for the drafting of the Convention on Preventing and Combatting Violence against Women and Domestic Violence (Istanbul Convention).

Lynette J. Chua is Associate Professor of Law at the National University of Singapore and Yale-NUS College. She is a sociolegal scholar and the author of *The Politics of Rights and Southeast Asia* (2022), *The Politics of Love in Myanmar: LGBT Mobilization and Human Rights as a Way of Life* (2018), and *Mobilizing Gay Singapore: Rights and Resistance in an Authoritarian State* (2014).

Rebecca Lock has a master's in human rights from University College London and has worked in various human rights, environmental, and development NGOs. She now works as the Senior Adviser to the Chief Executive at the Environment Agency in England, where she is an expert consultant in matters related to climate justice.

César Rodríguez-Garavito is Professor of Clinical Law and Chair of the Center for Human Rights and Global Justice at New York University School of Law. He is the editor-in-chief of *Open Global Rights.* He has been a visiting professor at Stanford, Brown, the University of Melbourne, European University Institute, University of Pretoria, the Getulio Vargas Foundation (Brazil), and the Andean University of Quito. Rodríguez-Garavito has served as expert witness of the Inter-American Court of Human Rights, an Adjunct Judge of the Constitutional Court of Colombia, a member of the Science Panel for the Amazon, and director of Dejusticia and the Center for Socio-Legal Research at Universidad de los Andes (Bogotá, Colombia). He has published numerous books and articles on global governance, international human rights, socio-environmental conflicts and movements, and climate change. His recent publications include *Litigating the Climate Emergency: How Human Rights, Courts and Legal Mobilization Can Bolster Climate Action* (ed., forthcoming).

Margaret Satterthwaite is a Professor of Clinical Law, Faculty Director of the Robert and Helen Bernstein Institute for Human Rights, and Co-Director of the Center for Human Rights and the Global Justice at New York University School of Law. Her research interests include legal empowerment, economic and social rights, methodological innovation in human rights, and the well-being of human rights advocates. Before joining the academy, she worked for a number of human rights organizations, including Amnesty International, Human Rights First, and the Commission Nationale de Verité et de Justice in Haiti. As Director of the Global Justice Clinic, she and her students partner with grassroots organizations and movements to prevent, challenge, and redress rights violations in situations of global inequality. She has worked as a consultant to numerous UN agencies and special rapporteurs and has served on the boards of several human rights organizations.

Lisa Vanhala is a Professor of Political Science at University College London. Her research and teaching focuses on human rights, environmental politics, and climate change governance. Her first book was *Making Rights a Reality? Disability Rights Activists and Legal Mobilization* (2011). She has recently published in *Comparative Political Studies, Global Environmental Politics, Global Environmental Change, Environmental Politics* and *Law & Policy*.

1

Legal Mobilization for Human Rights

An Introduction

Gráinne de Búrca

1. Changing the Emphasis of Human Rights Scholarship

There has been a recent turn in human rights scholarship, including in legal scholarship, from a previously dominant top-down focus on laws, institutions, and actors including human rights treaties, domestic and international courts and tribunals, and governmental officials, towards a more bottom-up focus on civil society activists, advocacy groups, affected communities, and social movements.

Law-focused human rights scholarship was long preoccupied with examining the enactment, implementation, and interpretation of human rights treaties, analysing the output of their monitoring mechanisms as well as the rulings of courts in human rights litigation, and appraising the activities of other domestic and international institutions such as special rapporteurs, the Human Rights Council and its predecessor, and international criminal tribunals. In more recent years, however, a growing number of legal scholars have been examining dimensions of the human rights field that had previously been more usually the domain of sociological, anthropological, and political science scholarship, including topics such as social movements, civil society activism, and the strategies of advocacy groups. Some of the recent interest in these subjects may have been sparked by the publication of an array of empirical and sociological studies examining the effectiveness or otherwise of human rights law in advancing rights in practice,[1] including a subset which pointed to the importance of domestic civil society as a factor.[2] In particular, influential work like that of Beth Simmons's book-length study, *Mobilizing for Human Rights*,[3] has attracted considerable interest from scholars within multiple disciplines, and legal academics too

[1] E.g. Hathaway, 'Do Human Rights Treaties Make a Difference?', 111 *Yale Law Journal* (2002) 1935; Hafner-Burton and Tsutsui, 'Human Rights in a Globalizing World: The Paradox of Empty Promises', 110 *American Journal of Sociology* (2005) 1373; Keith, 'The United Nations International Covenant on Civil and Political Rights: Does It Make a Difference in Human Rights Behavior?', 36 *Journal of Peace Research* (1999) 85; Hill, 'Estimating the Effects of Human Rights Treaties on State Behavior', 72 *Journal of Politics* (2010) 1161; Simmons, 'From Ratification to Compliance', in T. Risse, S. C. Ropp, and K. Sikkink (eds), *The Persistent Power of Human Rights* (2012); Fariss, 'Yes, Human Rights Practices are Improving Over Time', 113 *American Political Science Review* (2019) 868.

[2] See e.g. Neumayer, 'Do International Human Rights Treaties Improve Respect for Human Rights?', 49 *Journal of Conflict Resolution* (2005) 925; Englehart and Miller, 'The CEDAW Effect: International Law's Impact on Women's Rights', 13 *Journal of Human Rights* (2014) 22; J. Krommendijk, *The Domestic Impact and Effectiveness of State Reporting Under UN Human Rights Treaties in the Netherlands, New Zealand and Finland* (2014).

[3] B. Simmons, *Mobilizing for Human Rights* (2012).

Gráinne de Búrca, *Legal Mobilization for Human Rights* In: *Legal Mobilization for Human Rights*. Edited by: Gráinne de Búrca, Oxford University Press. © Gráinne de Búrca, 2022. DOI: 10.1093/oso/9780192866578.003.0001

have begun to investigate how and in what ways the actions of civil society advocates, affected communities, and social movements can activate, promote, and generate recognition of human rights. Margaret Keck and Kathryn Sikkink's book on transnational networks and their analysis of the 'boomerang' effect have also drawn the attention of legal scholars to the role of civil society activists.[4] Similarly, the work of Sally Engle Merry, a leading anthropology scholar, on what she has described as the vernacularization of human rights launched a fresh wave of legal and other research on the range of issues involved.[5] The insights generated by writers such as Simmons, Merry, Sikkink, and others have piqued the interest of human rights lawyers to look beyond legal texts and their interpretation, and beyond official legal and political institutions and elite actors to examine instead—or in addition—the activities of those whose rights are at stake, who mobilize to assert and claim their rights.

The term mobilization typically refers to activities which seek to raise awareness, to motivate and catalyse others into taking action collectively to achieve particular goals. Human rights mobilization refers to activities which are directed at encouraging and promoting collective action towards the protection and realization of human rights. While human rights are understood by many as pre-legal and moral claims to be asserted and argued for without necessarily invoking law or legal strategies, nevertheless mobilization for human rights often entails some kind of engagement with legal norms and institutions, and often with international or transnational norms and institutions. *Legal* mobilization for human rights in particular focuses on the use of law and legal norms, instruments, channels, and institutions as a means for advancing rights in practice. While legal mobilization clearly implicates human rights treaties and legislation, as well as courts and other relevant institutions, the scholarly turn to examine mobilization for human rights has gradually directed attention beyond the content of laws and the actions and output of courts to look more closely also at those who are motivated to assert and claim rights, to argue for their protection and realization, to organize and strategize about how and where to do so, how and to what extent to use legal strategies, and for what goals and outcomes to aim.

The importance of examining mobilization is not just that it draws attention to those whose rights are at issue, and whose empowerment or protection is at stake, but more centrally because of the fact that human rights remain an intangible ideal or an abstraction until they are claimed, pursued, and realized. And human rights law remains as text unless and until it is used to assert and advance the rights and interests of those it is supposed to protect, but who have been neglected, marginalized, dominated, or oppressed. Human rights treaties are clearly not self-enforcing, and are at best selectively invoked and enforced by domestic and international elites, who are motivated and constrained by a range of political interests and considerations. The strongest impetus for claiming, activating, and enforcing human rights comes from 'below', from those whose lives are adversely affected by disempowerment, domination, or deprivation, even as they invoke international and domestic laws and institutions, or

[4] M. Keck and K. Sikkink, *Activists Beyond Borders: Advocacy Networks in International Politics* (1998).

[5] See e.g. S. Engle Merry, *Human Rights and Gender Violence: Translating International Law into Local Justice* (2006). See also M. Goodale and S. Engle Merry, *The Practice of Human Rights: Tracking Law Between the Local and the Global* (2003).

draw on the engagement or support of international and domestic actors and agencies to do so.[6]

None of this is to say that the study of top-down or elite actors and institutions in the human rights field is necessarily less relevant or important than the study of social movements and activists, particularly not during an era in which the lens of scholarly analysis is increasingly being trained on the Western and colonial origins, as well as hegemonic practices and selective uses of international human rights law. At the same time, bottom-up analysis of legal mobilization reveals a different and often overlooked dimension, in particular the ways in which human rights are activated and used for emancipatory purposes by communities and their advocates to challenge the ways in which their lives are limited or dominated by denial of their rights.

The study of legal mobilization for human rights engages a potentially wide range of issues including the causes, modalities, and consequences of mobilization. One such set of questions concerns who exactly claims rights and pursues them using legal strategies, whether it is groups of individuals and communities who are actually affected, or wider social movements, or specialized advocates or organizations mobilizing on their behalf, and what rights they mobilize to protect. A second set of questions concerns what strategies and tools are used, what forums are chosen, and the extent to which particular mobilization strategies are likely to be effective, as well as what seem to be the probable determinants of successful campaigns, and why certain arguments, approaches, and goals are pursued rather than others. A third set of questions concerns the range of obstacles to human rights mobilization as well as the likelihood and extent of counter-mobilization. Comparative approaches raise questions as to why human rights mobilization is possible or successful in certain contexts, and why particular strategies are possible or successful in certain contexts, and under certain conditions but not in others. Several key aspects of these questions are addressed in the chapters which follow in this collection.

2. The Contributions to this Collection

Lynette Chua's focus is on LGBTQ+ mobilization in the context of authoritarian systems, looking at the kinds of constraints which are imposed on LGBTQ groups in authoritarian contexts as well as how they nonetheless mobilize around human rights, and what emerges from such mobilization.[7] Christine Chinkin examines a rather different but also highly challenging context for human rights mobilization around issues of gender violence and conflict, namely the attempt to shift consideration of these issues beyond the forum of international human rights bodies to the more politically powerful UN Security Council.[8] Rebecca Lock and Lisa Vanhala scrutinize a layer of professional civil society advocacy situated between grassroots groups on the one hand and governmental and international institutions on the other, to reflect on the reasons

[6] For an analysis of the relationship between social movements and human rights, see N. Stammers, *Human Rights and Social Movements* (2009).

[7] L. J. Chua, 'LGBTQ Rights Mobilization and Authoritarianism', in this volume.

[8] C. Chinkin, 'Women, Peace, and Security: A Human Rights Agenda?', in this volume.

why certain prominent NGOs adopted a human rights framework to address climate change while others did not.[9] In the final two chapters, César Rodríguez-Garavito, Carlos Baquero-Díaz, and Margaret Satterthwaite reflect on the transformative potential of genuinely grassroots human rights mobilization. Rodríguez-Garavito and Baquero-Díaz describe how the Sarakayu people of Ecuador mobilized not so much to *invoke* international human rights law to advance their cause as to *reshape* international human rights law and to bring their understanding of the rights of nature and of their community to bear on existing domestic and international law and policy.[10] Building on the theme of Rodríguez-Garavito and Baquero-Díaz, Margaret Satterthwaite addresses a fundamental question regarding all kinds of human rights advocacy, namely whether the idea of mobilization for human rights can itself be transformed so as to ensure not just that the rights of disempowered communities and individuals are advanced through law, but also more fundamentally to empower those communities to build their own movements, direct their own advocacy, and demand responsiveness to the claims they identify for themselves.[11] She describes this kind of transformation of legal mobilization as critical legal empowerment.

Beginning with her analysis of LGBTQ mobilization, Lynette Chua considers the constraints which the authoritarian context imposes on the possibilities for rights mobilization. One of the significant contributions of her analysis is to draw attention to the spectrum of authoritarian domination, and to the fact that such contexts exist not only within politically authoritarian states, but in all kinds of political systems in which forms of societal authoritarianism are at work. Drawing attention to the ways in which domination is exercised over particular groups or individuals by those occupying a hierarchical social position, she describes societal authoritarianism as existing where those who are in a position of power and authority maintain control through both legal and non-legal means over those perceived as threatening to their authority, with a view to preventing the latter from altering their circumstances and the status quo of relations. Understood in this way, many subordinated social groups—religious minorities, women in patriarchal societies, prisoners, refugees, specific ethnic groups, among many others—in different contexts experience a form of societal authoritarianism. Or as Chua describes it, 'authoritarianism is all over', even if it is more dominant, widespread, and entrenched in some contexts than others. Nevertheless, she argues, just as authoritarianism can structure and mould the nature, extent, and possibilities of mobilization for rights, so also can mobilization for rights at times alter the conditions and structures of authoritarianism.

Drawing on research into LGBTQ+ activism in Singapore and Myanmar, Chua examines the set of political and other restrictions that are imposed on mobilization for rights, including limits on assembly, association, and speech, as well as threats of imprisonment and restrictions on funding and resources, along with non-legal restrictions such as violence and intimidation. Taking these together with the set of

[9] R. Lock and L. Vanhala, 'International NGOs and the (Non) Mobilization of Human Rights in the Context of Climate Change: An Inconvenient Frame?', in this volume.

[10] C. Rodríguez-Garavito and C. A. Baquero-Díaz, 'Reframing Indigenous Rights: The Right to Consultation and the Rights of Nature and Future Generations in the Sarayaku Legal Mobilization', in this volume.

[11] M. Satterthwaite, 'Critical Legal Empowerment for Human Rights', in this volume.

authoritarian conditions which are directed not at any kind of rights mobilization but particularly at LGBTQ+ activism, she notes an array of targeted measures which restrict education and information, and which use pretexts to conduct raids on gay business and other venues, and which use laws on public order, safety, or 'decency' to limit and control LGBTQ+ individuals and communities. These combined sets of general and targeted restrictions do not, she tells us, prevent LGBTQ+ mobilization, even though they certainly constrain and shape it. Chua describes how, in addition to the familiar tactics of domestic, regional, and international litigation, lobbying, and letter-writing, LGBTQ+ groups use informal and sometimes underground methods of consciousness-raising, gathering, grievance articulation, and collective identity-building through creative forms of protest or parade that—like the Singapore Pink Dot gatherings—have managed to avoid governmental restrictions. She identifies the range of instrumental gains, including decriminalization, legal protection, access to benefits and services, and the catalysation of further mobilization, as well as the creation of resonance and building networks of support through LGBTQ+ mobilization. But she also highlights the crucial symbolic gains, including the sense of self as well as collective identity that can develop for LGBTQ+ persons when they overcome what for many has been a societally induced sense of shame and fear, to mobilize for recognition of their rights. She concludes by addressing some of the critiques of rights discourse and rights mobilization as a strategy both in general as well as for LGBTQ+ communities in particular, including that they are ineffectual or even harmful—individualistic, deradicalizing and Western-dominated—in pursuing social change. While acknowledging some of these and other risks, she argues that rights strategies which may seem dated and unimaginative to those who are used to conditions of political freedom can be powerful for activists struggling in authoritarian contexts. She concludes by reminding us of the contingent and contextual relationship between rights mobilization and authoritarianism in different political, social, and legal contexts.

Christine Chinkin in her chapter then addresses the move by gender activists to shift the focus of their mobilization from traditional human rights forums such as the treaty-body committees that monitor human rights treaty implementation, to the less promising, more militarized and patriarchal but also considerably more powerful UN Security Council. She questions, as the title of her contribution intimates, whether the Women, Peace and Security (WPS) agenda that was first formally introduced by the Security Council in Resolution 1325 of 2000 can really be thought of as a human rights agenda. She traces the antecedents of the WPS agenda in much earlier women's social movements, identifying the move to include a Women's Charter in the Versailles Treaty as a key moment as women struggled for recognition of their political, participatory, and economic rights, for working women's rights, and for peace and disarmament. Chinkin describes the World Conference on Human Rights in Vienna and the Beijing World Conference on women as well as the Cairo conference in the 1990s as key events which supplemented the earlier adoption of the Convention on the Elimination of All Forms of Discrimination against Women (CEDAW), and at which women activists sought to highlight both the continuum of gender-based violence from peacetime to armed conflict, as well as the need to challenge the traditional divide between the applicability of human rights to peacetime and humanitarian law to armed conflict. But she shows that gender and sexuality remained controversial topics, and how subsequent peace negotiations—including after the Yugoslav war—made little reference to women. This was the stage at which women's activists began to shift attention to the Security Council as a possible forum for advancing women's rights, particularly with regard to participation and ending impunity for sexual violence during conflict. Chinkin examines the evolution of the WPS agenda from the first resolution adopted by the Security Council in 2000 through to the tenth resolution adopted in 2019. She observes the way the agenda gained political weight but no additional legal force through the use of the Security Council as a forum, and traces how the human rights standards articulated in CEDAW were given a lower profile in some of the resolutions than in others, and indeed were diluted in some of them. Even at the high point of the WPS agenda in 2015, she notes that human rights featured only weakly—with little reference to CEDAW or any of the other relevant human rights treaties governing the entitlement of survivors of sexual violence and others—and that the language of security and humanitarianism predominate. She points to the way the WPS agenda has been strategically linked by states to concerns such as counter-terrorism and counter-extremism, in a way that neglects and even endangers the rights of women, and notes that the Security Council did not seek the assistance or experience of the human rights treaty bodies, even though CEDAW in particular has been developing its own rights-based WPS agenda.

Nevertheless, Chinkin points more positively to certain institutional innovations bringing the human rights agenda of the treaty bodies and the security and conflict agenda of the UNSC closer together, and importantly, she suggests that having the Security Council engaged in the WPS agenda has helped during the recent global backlash against women's rights. In particular, certain language in the 2019 resolutions reaffirms the commitments to sexual and reproductive rights from the resolutions adopted in earlier years, despite vocal opposition from the Trump administration and others. One of her observations is that mobilization by women around the Security Council and the WPS agenda today is less about *advancing* women's rights than it is about resisting the widespread and powerful backlash against gender equality taking place around the world. Significantly, however, in terms of mobilization 'from below', she points to the fact that attempts to bring civil society into the Security Council's activity—for example by inviting women from conflict-affected territories to brief the Council on specific contexts—have not been particularly successful. Yet despite the many problems associated with trying to move a women's rights agenda into a militaristic and state-centric forum, Chinkin concludes there are human rights entry points in the Security Council's resolutions and that civil society actors should mobilize around them, engaging with both the human rights mechanisms and with the Security Council.

Rebecca Lock and Lisa Vanhala's chapter, like certain aspects of Christine Chinkin's, examines the coming together of two different agendas that had previously been rather separately pursued—those of human rights advocacy and climate change action. In seeking to answer the question of why some key NGOs began to mobilize around the connections between human rights and climate change while others did not, they study five large international NGOs—two human rights organizations, two environmental organizations, and one development organization—to examine the extent to which they have linked these two agendas. They find that while Oxfam and

Greenpeace led the way in combining both frames at an early stage and Greenpeace later maintained the lead, the two human rights organizations, Amnesty International and Human Rights Watch, were much more reluctant to do so or to address climate change until considerably later, and that the World Wildlife Fund hardly did so at all. In fact, while the authors present their chapter as addressing one overarching question, namely 'why do some INGOs mobilize human rights to address climate change whereas others do not', there are in fact a number of different strands contained within it. The first concerns whether, and if so why, human rights organizations (Amnesty, Human Rights Watch) did or did not address climate change, and a second concerns whether, and if so why, environmental organizations (Greenpeace, WWF) did or did not use a human rights approach to address climate change. The question applies rather differently again to Oxfam, given that it is neither a human rights organization nor an environmental one, but a development organization which chose to take the lead in using a human rights framework to address issues of climate change.

Drawing on both documentary analysis and interviews, Lock and Vanhala examine a set of proposed explanations for the varying choices of these different organizations. They begin by challenging the assumption in existing literature on international NGOs which suggests that the decision whether or not to adopt a human rights approach to climate justice depends on the degree of 'fit' with the NGO's substantive, ethical, tactical, and organizational features. They argue instead that it is the *perception* or *portrayal* by NGO staff of these features rather than the actual features themselves that influence the choice and extent of engagement. They identify a silo mentality within certain NGOs—possibly based on a perceived humility about the limits of staff expertise—which views certain issues as within the organization's 'turf' and others as outside it. Staff also identified a desire to adhere to what they understand to be their existing organizational mandate, to remain faithful to their roots and traditions, and not to stretch themselves too thin, as reasons for avoiding engagement with a human rights–climate change framework.

A second set of explanations given for the choices of organizations to engage or not with the human rights–climate change framework included the tactics used by the organization, or the strategy necessitated by their organizational structure. For example, the membership structure of Amnesty and WWF meant that the views of their supporters was an important consideration in deciding whether or not to engage with that framework. The nature, scale, and complexity of climate change also apparently made some within these organizations consider it too daunting for them to take on. The fact that Amnesty's work, for example, traditionally relied on a search for an identifiable perpetrator, a specific victim, and on the tactics of 'naming and shaming' were also factors which made the organization reluctant to address the climate change issue. Nevertheless, difference in tactics were not enough to explain the divergent positions taken by Oxfam, WWF, Amnesty, and Human Rights Watch in relation to human rights and climate change.

Lock and Vanhala also dismiss explanations based on the resources of the organizations or attributes of climate change as an issue. Ultimately the authors argue that perhaps the most important factor to account for the different approaches of the different organizations was the extent to which their staff pushed for change, and this in turn depended in part on whether the staff saw the organization's identity as fixed or evolving, whether they were willing to train existing staff or to recruit new staff with appropriate climate/human rights expertise, and whether they were willing to 'bridge frames', link new issues, and work on communicating the difficult messages around climate change.

Moving away from the professional advocacy organizations studied by Lock and Vanhala to focus on a grassroots human rights movement, César Rodríguez-Garavito and Carlos Andrés Baquero-Díaz examine how the Sarayaku Indigenous people mobilized over a ten-year period to challenge the attempts of the Ecuador government to authorize oil exploitation on their land. They describe how the trailblazing Sarayaku campaign challenged various aspects of existing international legal doctrines and procedures governing the rights of Indigenous peoples by insisting on a substantive definition of 'free prior and informed consent' (FPIC) based on self-determination rather than mere consultation, also by invoking the rights of nature and the rights of future generations, and by bringing a long-term perspective that has not been typical of strategic litigation and human rights mobilization. Rather as Lock and Vanhala examined the willingness or reluctance of a range of NGOs to 'bridge frames' and to combine a human rights approach with climate change, Rodríguez-Garavito and Baquero-Díaz describe how the Sarayaku created a new and ultimately powerful bridge between the Indigenous rights frame, the human rights frame, and the emergent frame of global action against climate change. And while conventional success—in terms of having the substantive definition of FPIC widely accepted as the international standard—has not (yet) been the outcome of their campaign, nevertheless they have succeeded in challenging the purely procedural consultation approach and in having a hybrid approach adopted by the Inter-American Court of Human Rights, and in part by the Bolivian government and the Colombian judiciary. Similarly, while their attempt to challenge the developmentalist agenda of the Ecuador political and corporate establishment and its subordination of environmental and Indigenous rights to the economic promotion of extractive industries, did not succeed and Indigenous leaders were subject to harassment, nevertheless they succeeded in stopping multiple attempts to drill for oil in their territory. And, equally importantly, the authors suggest that the metrics for judging the successes of the Sarayaku mobilization should include the extent to which they have brought about a counter-hegemonic reinterpretation of international rules on free prior and informed consent, and a change in the way relevant legal concepts and rights are understood. In particular, a major long-term goal of their campaign was to bring about an ecocentric reframing of their dispute, to assert and gain legal recognition of their Amazonian territory as a living rainforest, and a subject of rights in itself. Despite the difficulties they faced domestically, their legal mobilization has had important global ramifications of a longer-term kind for the rights of Indigenous peoples, for the rights of nature, and for the climate action movement.

In the final chapter in the volume, Margaret Satterthwaite builds on the bottom-up perspective adopted by Rodríguez-Garavito and Baquero-Díaz and makes a powerful argument that advocates, lawyers, and activists should follow the leadership of those who are suffering injustice, rather than aiming to lead them. She takes the language of the UN project of 'legal empowerment of the poor', which seeks to help those who are excluded and marginalized to access law and legal remedies (with particular focus on property rights, business regulation, and the formal justice system), and suggests a critical reorientation of that concept to put those who are affected by injustice to the forefront and in the lead. Drawing inspiration from Sally Engle Merry's ideas of vernacularization, on 'subaltern cosmopolitanism' in the work of Boaventura de Sousa Santos, and on 'movement lawyering' in the US, she argues that it is necessary to shift the focus away from elite institutions and actors and to examine and support the ways communities and movements themselves are using legal empowerment to address the impact of global injustice. She gives the examples of community paralegals in Kenya and Haiti, community justice workers as health advocates in Mozambique, community-based monitoring of core socio-economic rights in Delhi, monitoring and 'groundtruthing' by villagers challenging coal mining impacts in Odisha, community-based strategic litigation in South Africa and Haiti, and the accompaniment of immigrants who are targeted for deportation and detention, to elucidate a critical legal empowerment approach which aims to build grassroots power. She uses an in-depth case study of the work of an Indigenous community in Guyana, the Wapichan people of the Southern Rupununi, to illustrate how this community empowered itself through a process of intensive participatory research to identify and articulate customary norms concerning the tenure of land and the use and management of biological resources within their territory, in order to engage on their own terms with national and international law on the issues. They also undertook a process of participatory mapping of their territory and used these community-generated maps to carry out environmental monitoring and to curb unlawful mining and logging on the land. Finally, the Wapichan community sought to shape the law and to reform the laws of Guyana that had dispossessed and disadvantaged them, engaging in the kind of legal innovation that the Sarayaku in Ecuador similarly used in their mobilization to protect the rainforest. The kind of critical legal empowerment Satterthwaite is both describing and arguing for is one that requires human rights advocacy to be not just rights-based, but also movement-centred and accountable to the community, led not by external legal norms and standards but by the activism and struggles of the rights-holders and by their own leadership.

3. Emergent Themes

The key themes around legal mobilization for human rights to emerge from the chapters in this collection are therefore: first, the continuing resilience and importance of the idea of human rights, particularly to communities that are repressed, dominated, or marginalized; second, the ways in which political and societal authoritarianism, and other political and social structures shape and limit (but do not necessarily exclude) the opportunities for effective mobilization; third, the importance of the choice of fora for seeking to bring about change and the advantages and disadvantages of different kinds of forum; fourth, the role intermediary actors such as leading NGOs can play in thinking innovatively and being willing to 'bridge frames' and reorient strategies to address pressing challenges; fifth, the possibilities for subaltern mobilization to reshape human rights law not just to address their realities but also so as to transform international legal understandings and key concepts; and finally, the importance of supporting genuinely community-led legal mobilization.

The account of the struggles of members of the LGBTQ+ community within authoritarian states and the creative and innovative ways they manage despite multiple barriers and constraints to assemble, to assert their identity and their right to exist without being punished or silenced, reminds us that at least some of the critiques of 'rights talk' as depoliticizing, ineffectual, or harmful may be inapt for authoritarian contexts. Similarly, Chua's insights as to the less often acknowledged but unquestionable prevalence of societal and not just political authoritarianism and the way it represses and controls particular groups and communities, points to the possibly wider applicability of that reminder beyond the LGBTQ+ community and beyond authoritarian states. Her contribution points to the empowering potential of rights mobilization, even in the face of very significant obstacles and risks.

The mixed record of success of the WPS agenda in including women in the peacebuilding process and bringing a gender perspective to bear on international policymaking in relation to armed conflict and violence points to the importance of the choice of forum by activists when considering how best to promote the rights of women globally. While a human rights forum such as the CEDAW committee would be normatively speaking more persuasive and attractive than the UN Security Council, nevertheless the power and authority of the latter was considered by women's groups to be important to advance the agenda further. A more powerful and potentially more effective forum however presents its own challenges—in particular the UNSC's patriarchal character, its lack of engagement with or possible dilution of human rights standards, and relative inaccessibility to civil society. One of the strategies advocated by Christine Chinkin for managing the divergent advantages and weaknesses of these different international fora is to build synergies and institutional relationships between them, with a view to combining a rights-respecting gender perspective with political power and authority, particularly at a time of 'gender backlash' in many parts of the world.

The role of organizations like Amnesty, Human Rights Watch, and Oxfam are arguably insufficiently studied in the human rights literature. They act in many contexts as intermediary institutions between affected communities whose rights are at stake and governmental and international actors and institutions. In some cases influenced strongly by the preferences of their funders and in others by their membership, they select issues on which to campaign and causes for which to advocate. Many of the critiques of the human rights movement to date have effectively been critiques of the most prominent of these organizations, focusing on the selectivity of the issues they have addressed and in particular on their relatively weak showing in relation to socio-economic rights by comparison with their concern for civil and political rights.[12] Lock and Vanhala's analysis in this book shows how some of the major human rights organizations were unwilling or very slow to address the issue of climate change, despite its profound implications for the enjoyment of all kinds of human rights. The role of such well-resourced and well-positioned advocacy NGOs, including the issues they select and the strategies they adopt, are clearly important for the ways in which communities

[12] See e.g. S. Hopgood, *The Endtimes of Human Rights* (2013); S. Moyn, *Not Enough* (2018).

and issues are represented, and in influencing which human rights causes tend to be prioritized and promoted.

In an important recent contribution from a range of scholars and practitioners of human rights, Knuckey and others criticize 'disempowering advocacy models', which they define as forms of human rights practice in which outside advocates (not the rights-holders themselves, or those affected) "set social justice agendas, decide strategies, and conduct investigations and advocacy with no or limited input or direction from affected rights-holders or rightsholder-advocates".[13] They argue that top-down, disempowering advocacy of this kind can bring about results that don't meet the needs of rights-holders, and can produce backlash as well as security risks, while also undermining the development and power of local movements. They point to the fact that there are often power differentials between outsider-advocates and affected rights-holders, and they argue instead for what they call forms of 'critically responsive human rights practice' and provide examples and illustrations of supportive, participatory, and empowering advocacy.

The arguments of Knuckey and her co-authors resonate with the issues highlighted in Satterthwaite's and Rodríguez-Garavito and Baquero-Díaz's chapters, which include the importance of grassroots leadership not just in advocating for rights and presenting the issues faced by particular communities who have been disempowered and exploited, but also in terms of its capacity to reshape and reorient international human rights law, and to voice claims and priorities in their own vernacular. These final two chapters argue powerfully for and illustrate the importance and effectiveness of genuinely community-led human rights advocacy, rather than campaigns led primarily by professional organizations or determined by external funders and expert advisers. It is not just a matter of communities and affected groups localizing and vernacularizing international human rights law, and drawing from laws made and enforced by elites, but of these communities and constituencies creating and giving voice to their rights, shaping the making and interpretation of human rights law through their engagement.

The thrust of the contributions to this volume is to emphasize the importance to the overall human rights agenda of mobilization from below. But the heterogeneous nature of the key societal actors involved and the diverse means through which they engage and influence outcomes also serves to remind us that it is not a question of bottom up or top down, but rather of multiple and often carefully tailored forms of interaction and reinforcement. The shape of the international human rights regime is never settled; it always remains a work in practice. As one or other of the component parts becomes less innovative and less responsive to the demands on the ground, other parts will of necessity become more active and move to provide leadership. While there will always be a risk of key institutional actors, whether intergovernmental or non-governmental, becoming ineffectual, the same cannot be said of mobilization from below which will always take different forms and be highly responsive to changing circumstances.

[13] Knuckey *et al.*, 'Power in Human Rights Advocate and Rightsholder Relationships: Critiques, Reforms, and Challenges', 33 *Harvard Human Rights Journal* (2021) 1.

2
LGBTQ Rights Mobilization and Authoritarianism

*Lynette J. Chua**

1. Introduction

Since the middle of the last century, individuals and groups have increasingly advocated for the rights of sexual and gender minorities, what is now widely known as LGBTQ rights (lesbian, gay, bisexual, transgender, and queer).[1] The number of academic writings about LGBTQ rights has also increased, reflecting the growing interest in and importance of the subject matter.[2] These writings sometimes critique the failure of recalcitrant states to honour LGBTQ rights and the draconian measures imposed on sexual and gender minorities. Other times, they focus on the trials and tribulations of activists in regimes that readers would likely regard as liberal, as well as regimes that they would be more inclined to describe as authoritarian.

In this chapter, I examine the connections between LGBTQ rights mobilization and authoritarianism by considering the following aspects: the definition of LGBTQ rights mobilization; the definition and scope of authoritarianism, and the effects of authoritarian conditions on the emergence of LGBTQ rights mobilization; the strategies and tactics of LGBTQ rights mobilization under authoritarian conditions; and the consequences of LGBTQ rights mobilization. To explain each aspect, I am going to illustrate with examples from my ethnographic studies of LGBTQ rights mobilization in Singapore[3] and Myanmar,[4] as well as other research, news articles, and human rights reports on different parts of the world.

* I would like to thank Gráinne de Búrca and the Academy of European Law for the opportunity to write this chapter, and fellow participants and discussants at the March 2020 workshop, New York University, for their comments on the draft.

[1] The use of this term can be controversial due to the criticisms that I explore in Section 5. Usually, in my own work, I use this term or related terms, such as 'gay rights', if the activists in my study adopt the reference.

[2] A search of all databases and dates in HeinOnline shows a steady rise in the number of articles containing the phrase, 'LGBT* right', 'gay right', or 'lesbian right' in the title or full text since the mid-2000s. Collective mobilization of LGBTQ rights has increasingly received attention from scholars of social movements over the past 25 years: Ghaziani *et al.*, 'Cycles of Sameness and Difference in LGBT Social Movements', 42 *Annual Review of Sociology (ARS)* (2016) 165.

[3] Chua, 'Pragmatic Resistance, Law, and Social Movements in Authoritarian States: The Case of Gay Collective Action in Singapore', 46 *Law and Society Review (LSR)* (2012) 713; L. J. Chua, *Mobilizing Gay Singapore: Rights and Resistance in an Authoritarian State* (2014); Chua, 'Rights Mobilization and the Campaign to Decriminalize Homosexuality in Singapore', 1 *Asian Journal of Law and Society (AJLS)* (2014) 205–228; Chua, 'Collective Litigation and Constitutional Challenges to Decriminalize Homosexuality in Singapore', 44 *Journal of Law & Society (JLS)* (2017) 433.

[4] Chua, 'The Vernacular Mobilization of Human Rights in Myanmar's Sexual Orientation and Gender Identity Movement', 49 *LSR* (2015) 299; Chua, 'Negotiating Social Norms and Relations in the

Lynette J. Chua, *LGBTQ Rights Mobilization and Authoritarianism* In: *Legal Mobilization for Human Rights*. Edited by: Gráinne de Búrca, Oxford University Press. © Gráinne de Búrca and Lynette J. Chua, 2022. DOI: 10.1093/oso/9780192866578.003.0002

As a sociolegal scholar, I approach the subject of LGBTQ rights mobilization and authoritarianism based on the scholarship's established tradition of legal mobilization research. I do not focus on the development of jurisprudence related to LGBTQ rights, or normative or theoretically abstract arguments about LGBTQ rights. Rather, I am concerned about LGBTQ rights mobilization and authoritarianism as social phenomena that are to be explained and understood from empirical data and analysis.

2. What Is LGBTQ Rights Mobilization?

I start with the question of what LGBTQ rights mobilization entail, rather than the subject matter—LGBTQ rights—because LGBTQ rights and their implications emerge from mobilization. Certainly, one way to understand LGBTQ rights is to look to formal legal instruments and international documents such as the Yogyakarta Principles on the Application of International Human Rights Law in relation to Sexual Orientation and Gender Identity (Yogyakarta Principles) and United Nations resolutions.[5] These documents extend the general corpus of human rights to sexuality and gender. From this perspective, LGBTQ rights encompass such civil–political rights as expression, assembly, association, and personal security, and such socio-economic and cultural rights as employment, housing, education, and healthcare. Another approach, often adopted by non-profit organizations in their reports, is to classify LGBTQ rights into issues, such as decriminalization of consensual same-sex relations, legal protection from discrimination and violence, and legal recognition of relationships and non-heteronormative or non-conforming gender identities.[6]

In reality, the contents of LGBTQ rights vary in importance and development across jurisdictions. Where there are still anti-sodomy laws, decriminalization is a priority for activists. Furthermore, whether decriminalization is a matter of right to privacy, equality, or life and liberty, depends on the strategy and audience. In court, activists and their lawyers would want to tailor their arguments to suit the jurisprudence of the jurisdiction in question, be it domestic or supranational. But they may change their arguments, their emphases, or even their tone, when they appear before politicians, international agencies, supporters, or opponents.

Micromobilization of Human Rights: The Case of Burmese Lesbian Activism', 41 *Law & Social Inquiry (LSI)* (2016) 643; L. J. Chua, *The Politics of Love in Myanmar: LGBT Mobilization and Human Rights as a Way of Life* (2019).

[5] E.g. *Report of the United Nations High Commissioner for Human Rights, Discriminatory Laws and Practices and Acts of Violence against Individuals based on their Sexual Orientation and Gender Identity*, UN GAOR, Hum. Rts. Council, 19th Sess., UN Doc. A/HRC/19/41 (17 Nov. 2011); *Human Rights Council Resolution—Human Rights, Sexual Orientation and Gender Identity*, UN GAOR, Hum. Rts. Council, 27th Sess., UN Doc. A/HRC/RES/27/3 (26 Sept. 2014); *Protection against Violence and Discrimination based on Sexual Orientation and Gender Identity*, UN GAOR, Hum. Rts. Council, 32nd Sess., UN Doc. A/HRC/RES/32/2 (30 June 2016).

[6] Chua, 'LGBTQ Rights Litigation: A Singaporean Case Study', in D. Law (ed.), *Constitutionalism in Context* (forthcoming); A. Carroll and L. R. Mendos, *State Sponsored Homophobia 2017: A World Survey of Sexual Orientation Laws: Criminalisation, Protection and Recognition* (2017).

In other words, LGBTQ rights take shape from multidirectional, ongoing conversations, collaborations, and contestations among activists from the same organizations and across groups with different orientations and goals, with their supporters and allies, as well as with or against the state and other opponents. Hence, the meanings of LGBTQ rights come from the ground, from what their advocates want to achieve with rights—if they do turn to rights—and how they use rights through their social interactions to achieve those goals. Even if few resort to rights due to high levels of repression, the lack and constraints of mobilization in and of themselves inform the meanings of LGBTQ rights.

What, then, is LGBTQ rights mobilization? I offer the following explanation based on widely accepted definitions of legal mobilization in sociolegal literature:[7] LGBTQ rights mobilization refers to the individual or collective use of rights to express a grievance, desire, or demand for persons who identify as sexual or gender minorities. As a form of rights practice, it involves making sense of and putting rights into action to ward off attacks, defeat restrictions, and make gains, seek entry into, or change existing legal or social institutions.[8] LGBTQ rights mobilization, therefore, does not necessarily invoke the law in formal legal institutions, such as the courts. It includes making verbal appeals to rights, such as portraying as rights violations experiences of being discriminated because of one's sexuality or gender identity.

LGBTQ rights mobilization is composed of a series of political processes involving interactions between two types of conditions. One type is structural. They include conditions that shape the openness of society and state to non-heteronormativity and gender non-conformity, as well as conditions that facilitate or constrain LGBTQ rights activism. The other type is subjective, such as identities, social positions, and interests and desires that come with those identities and positions, which influence the manner in which social actors interpret and respond to structural conditions. A lesbian may interpret a law or court decision differently from a transgender woman, transgender man, or gay man; a lesbian who is also an ethnic minority may interpret the same court decision differently from a lesbian who belongs to the dominant ethnic group; the reactions of a lesbian, a gay man, or transgender person may also contrast greatly with that of a cisgender, heterosexual person strongly opposed to homosexuality.

The social actors who engage in LGBTQ rights mobilization include activists and claimants of LGBTQ rights, state actors, and opponents of LGBTQ rights. Social actors put structural and subjective conditions in interaction, giving rise to the political processes of LGBTQ rights mobilization. Subjective conditions shift as social actors move across different contexts and encounter different structural factors and other actors. A lesbian activist, for example, socializes in multiple settings such as a

[7] Lempert, 'Mobilizing Private Law: An Introductory Essay', 11 *LSR* (1976) 173; Zemans, 'Legal Mobilization: The Neglected Role of the Law in the Political System', 77 *American Political Science Review* (1983) 690; M. W. McCann, *Rights at Work: Pay Equity Reform and the Politics of Legal Mobilization* (1994); Chua, 'Legal Mobilization and Authoritarianism', 15 *Annual Review of Law and Social Science (ARLSS)* (2019) 355. 'Rights mobilization' and 'legal mobilization' are often conflated in socio-legal literature. For the most part, the two concepts are interchangeable. However, 'legal mobilization' is arguably the broader of the two, especially in cases when the law is mobilized without specific reference to rights, for example, when using a criminal provision to prosecute somebody.

[8] McCann (n. 7); Chua (n. 7).

close-knit group of fellow lesbian activists, a coalition of activists made up diverse sexual and gender minorities, her natal family, and her co-workers. The interactions between structural and subjective conditions not only produce meanings for LGBTQ rights but also reshape the very conditions of structure and subjectivity themselves.

In the political processes of LGBTQ rights mobilization, social actors employ rights as though they are malleable resources. They rely on the instrumental power of rights, the direct capacity of rights to effect changes in the form of remedies and protections in formal law, such as the enactment of anti-discrimination legislation, the legal recognition of same-sex families, or the striking down of laws that penalize consensual same-sex relations. But, more than that, these actors draw upon the connotative power of rights, the discursive, strategic, and symbolic capacity of rights.[9] For example, activists strategically frame the grievances of sexual and gender minorities as being about LGBTQ *rights* and speak the language of rights to win allies and secure funding. Other times, they depict rights as a symbol of equality and dignity in their attempts to change the way people think about their plight, and the social status of sexual and gender minorities.

3. Authoritarianism and Emergence of LGBTQ Rights Mobilization

Authoritarian conditions conjure up images of violent quashing of dissent. Can LGBTQ rights mobilization occur under authoritarian conditions? Sociolegal scholarship, social movements studies, and other disciplines in the social sciences show that it can indeed occur despite, and perhaps because of, authoritarianism. The more interesting question is *how* structural conditions of authoritarianism obstruct and influence the emergence of LGBTQ rights mobilization.

To address this question, I want to take a step back to think about the definition and scope of authoritarianism first. The curbing of civil–political freedoms, quelling of opposition, and lack of choice over political leadership typically come to mind as features of authoritarian *states*. However, as I conducted more and more fieldwork on LGBTQ rights mobilization[10] and reconsidered the legal mobilization literature, I started to rethink this familiar association of authoritarianism with nation states, formal state institutions, and state actors. In an essay examining the place of authoritarianism in the study of legal mobilization, I proposed the following definition:

> [Authoritarianism] is the domination over a particular hierarchy of social relations by individuals or a group of people occupying the hierarchy's top rungs. To maintain those social relations and perpetuate the ensuing privileges, the individuals or group continuously exert power to extract conformity and order, through direct

[9] Goodale, 'The Power of Right(s): Tracking Empires of Law and New Modes of Social Resistance in Bolivia (and Elsewhere)', in M. Goodale, and S. E. Merry (eds), *The Practice of Human Rights: Tracking Law between the Global and the Local* (2007) 130; S. E. Merry *et al.*, 'Law from Below: Women's Human Rights and Social Movements in New York City', 44 *LSR* (2010) 101.

[10] See notes 3 and 4.

> and indirect means, from all or most segments of population within the hierarchy. In other words, the essence of authoritarianism is the possession and preservation of power of and by dominant individuals and groups. Achieving and maintaining power, consequently, compel the powerful to control those perceived as threatening to their authority so that they cannot or do not take action to alter their circumstances and the status quo arrangement of relations.[11]

The types of social control that achieve and maintain power range from the obvious to the imperceptible such that those subordinated are incognizant of their effects. The range includes: patent violence, threats, and coercion; extralegal and illegal measures; limited legal channels that offer opportunities for dissent and redress while protecting status quo interests; regulation of information, discourse, and behaviour to enforce certain ideologies and ways of life, and possibly normalize them.

Based on this definition, authoritarian powers emanate from multiple coexisting sites, formal state structures as well as religious communities, tribes, political parties, corporations, gangs, social clubs, and clans. Some sites of power overlap and interrelate. Some contradict and work in opposition to one another. All of them are authoritarian if the dominant group or individuals carry out targeted violence or discrimination, refuse to take action against those who perpetrated such acts, deny rights to all or targeted populations, or manage the social relations and associations of different populations.[12]

Just as the lines between democratic and non-democratic states are blurry and exist along a scale,[13] authoritarianism exists in shades and tones, and assumes a wide range of regimes: nation states; authoritarian enclaves within states that are either authoritarian or liberal, including subnational territories, legal institutions, and other state institutions such as immigration, militaries, and prisons; and social spaces, such as school, families, offices, factories, and churches.[14] These regimes vary in their authoritarian features, social controls, and impact. For example, some nation states accommodate LGBTQ rights but contain authoritarian enclaves, such as religions communities, which marginalize sexual and gender minority populations. Activists who mobilize against such enclaves may be able to draw from the state's legal order for support. However, those who mobilize for LGBTQ rights in an authoritarian state would not be able to rely on the state for even the most basic liberal-democratic protections.

'Authoritarianism is all over'[15] does not dilute the rich differences in political, legal, or economic conditions among authoritarian regimes, or conflate the distinctions between state-based and societal-based authoritarianism. The features of each authoritarian regime would have to be empirically drawn out and analysed. By paying attention to the empirical realities of authoritarianism, this perspective instead emphasizes that authoritarian regimes are neither static nor monolithic. They could alter

[11] Chua (n. 7) 357.
[12] Ibid. 358.
[13] Varol, 'Stealth Authoritarianism', 100 *Iowa Law Review* (2015) 1673.
[14] Chua (n. 7) 358.
[15] Ibid. 357.

as a result of mobilization. In return, the structural conditions of authoritarian regimes could also mould the (non)emergence of mobilization responses.

More specifically, authoritarianism's connections to LGBTQ rights mobilization can be divided into two main types: (i) conditions that constrain rights activism, shaping the desire, ability, or willingness to take action; (ii) conditions that are directed at sexual and gender minorities, and ferment the grievances underlying the substantive claims of LGBTQ rights mobilization, for example, the criminalization of same-sex relations. Both types of conditions manifest in social controls that range from the overt to covert. Together, the different forms of social control have cumulative impact on the emergence of LGBTQ rights mobilization.

A. Authoritarian Conditions that Constrain Rights Mobilization

The most blatant forms of authoritarian controls include the use of illegal force or legal restrictions by state actors, extremist groups, or other LGBTQ rights opponents to obstruct activities that facilitate activism, such as meetings, demonstrations, and speaking out. In Singapore, outspoken activists and political opponents have been prosecuted for breaking stringent laws delimiting assembly, association, and speech.[16] During the Jim Crow era, civil rights activists in the southern states of the United States—an authoritarian enclave for minorities[17] —were also threatened with arrests and prosecution, not to mention bodily harm.[18] In Namibia, the government intimidated LGBTQ rights activists with arrest, imprisonment, and exile.[19] In Myanmar, patriarchs such as fathers, uncles, and brothers, often restrain lesbians' freedom of movement, hindering lesbian activists from gathering and expanding their groups.[20]

Posing dangers to personal safety, livelihood, or family, the mere existence of blatant controls can deter people from doing anything about their grievances. In authoritarian enclaves of factories or offices, workers may be reluctant to sue their superiors or employers for violating their rights, even if they are protected by law, because they fear the repercussions of being fired, demoted, or worse.[21] Members of religious institutions may be reluctant to expose wrongdoing, for fear of ostracization.[22] According to my study on Singapore, having seen other activists portrayed as troublemakers for acts of civil disobedience, many LGBTQ activists avoid illegal tactics, because they believe arrests and prosecutions would discredit their cause and cost them political legitimacy.[23]

[16] Chua, 'Pragmatic Resistance' (n. 3); Chua, *Mobilizing Gay Singapore* (n. 3).

[17] R. Mickey, *Paths Out of Dixie: The Democratization of Authoritarian Enclaves in America's Deep South, 1944–1972* (2015).

[18] Barkan, 'Legal Control of the Southern Civil Rights Movement', 49 *American Sociological Review* (1984) 552.

[19] Currier, 'Deferral of Legal Tactics: A Global LGBT Social Movement Organization's Perspective', in Barclay *et al.* (eds), *Queer Mobilizations: LGBT Activists Confront the Law* (2009) 21.

[20] Chua, 'Negotiating Social Norms' (n. 4); Chua, *The Politics of Love* (n. 4).

[21] E.g. K. Bumiller, *The Civil Rights Society: The Social Construction of Victims* (1988); C. R. Albiston, *Institutional Inequality and the Mobilization of the Family and Medical Leave Act: Rights on Leave* (2010).

[22] P. Ewick and M. W. Steinberg, *Beyond Betrayal: The Priest Sex Abuse Crisis, the Voice of the Faithful, and the Process of Collective Identity First Edition* (2019).

[23] Chua, *Mobilizing Gay Singapore* (n. 3).

Other social controls suppress activism by stifling material and human resources. In the Jim Crow–era example, local authorities arrested and detained large numbers of protestors, and wore down civil rights activists by forcing them to deplete funds and energy in court processes.[24] Faced with registration requirements and legal restrictions on foreign funding, activists of registered organizations in China are wary of advocating for human rights or politically sensitive issues.[25] In Myanmar before the political transition of 2011, because HIV/AIDS groups were unable to openly advocate for rights, they organized cisgender, non-heterosexual men and transgender women under the guise of public health. However, this limited approach led them to leave out lesbians and transgender men. When the LGBTQ rights movement blossomed in the 2010s, lesbian activism lagged behind that of cisgender, non-heterosexual men, and transgender women. Whereas the latter drew their leadership and experience from HIV/AIDS organizing, lesbian activism did not enjoy the same head start in knowledge and interpersonal connections. Moreover, natal families' patriarchal control of women's freedom of movement, described earlier, compounded the difficulties of lesbian activism.[26]

Overt forms of control contribute to the subtler forms, whose effects may not be easily apparent or obvious to the subordinated. Violence and legal actions taken against rights could suppress activism over time, subduing rights discourse and limiting access to information about rights, and potentially prevent the subjugated from appreciating the relevance of rights to their grievances. For instance, before joining the LGBTQ rights movement in Myanmar, few sexual and gender minorities knew about human rights. Most of them associated rights with state retaliation, things that got people into trouble.[27] Because few people assert or otherwise mobilize rights, to outsiders looking in, the discourse could be dismissed as lacking cultural resonance or relevance. In liberal states where there appears to be greater civil–political liberties, protestors nevertheless are required to follow rules and regulations on where and when they may demonstrate. This is a type of 'channelling' that allows room for dissent while obscuring repressive controls.[28] Over time, protestors, even in societies that seem to allow greater freedom of assembly, could eventually accept the restrictions without questioning them.[29]

Away from authoritarianism in formal state structures, social institutions such as family, marriage, gender, and religion can also be authoritarian enclaves exerting elusive forms of control. For example, victims of abuse or harassment often hesitate to take legal action because they believe it would be incompatible with their roles as mothers, wives, or daughters.[30] Sexual and gender minorities who seem to enjoy

[24] Barkan (n.18).

[25] T. Hildebrandt, *Social Organizations and the Authoritarian State in China* (2013); Chua and Hildebrandt, 'From Health Crisis to Rights Advocacy? HIV/AIDS and Gay Activism in China and Singapore', 25 *International J. of Voluntary and Nonprofit Organizations* (2014) 1583.

[26] Chua, 'Negotiating Social Norms' (n. 4); Chua, *The Politics of Love* (n. 4).

[27] Chua, 'Vernacular Mobilization' (n. 4); Chua, *The Politics of Love* (n. 4).

[28] Earl, 'Political Repression: Iron Fists, Velvet Gloves, and Diffuse Control', 37 *ARS* (2011) 261.

[29] L. A. Fernandez, *Policing Dissent: Social Control and the Anti-Globalization Movement* (2009).

[30] Morgan, 'Risking Relationships: Understanding the Litigation Choices of Sexually Harassed Women', 33 *LSR* (1999) 67; Merry, 'Rights Talk and the Experience of Law: Implementing Women's Human Rights to Protection from Violence', 25 *Human Rights Quarterly (HRQ)* (2003) 343.

tolerant families and social circles may be keeping quiet about the oppression of non-heterosexuality or gender non-conformity, in return for their personal freedom to live as they please. This is an unspoken and unquestioned understanding that the role of the 'deviant' is to keep their heads down and simply act otherwise as good members of family and society.[31]

B. Authoritarian Conditions Targeted at LGBTQ Populations

A common and overt type of oppression of LGBTQ populations is outright physical violence. The International Day Against Homophobia, Transphobia and Biphobia, and Transgender Day of Remembrance are annual events on 17 May and 20 November, respectively, that draw attention to the violence suffered by sexual and gender minorities. Commemorated worldwide in hundreds of cities, the two events show that outright physical violence can exist anywhere, regardless of whether the regime is an authoritarian state or enclave. The perpetrators against sexual and gender minorities include state actors, especially the police whose brutality is well documented by human rights organizations,[32] and family members and close intimates who beat, sexually assault, or expel them from home.[33]

State laws and regulations constitute another overt form of social control, which could, in turn, legitimize police brutality and vigilante violence against sexual and gender minorities. The United Kingdom and United States, among many states, had anti-sodomy laws that were used to threaten and blackmail gay men.[34] Their legal institutions of marriage were authoritarian enclaves that excluded non-heterosexual people and denied their relationships and families legal recognition and protection. Militaries, such as those of the United States and South Korea, are arguably still enclaves against sexual and gender minorities within otherwise somewhat liberal regimes. In authoritarian states, LGBTQ authoritarian enclaves are arguably even worse. Russia's 'gay propaganda' law bans children and teens from access to information about sexual and gender minorities, preventing LGBTQ rights activists from providing assistance to the youth.[35] Many postcolonial governments of former British territories, such as Malaysia, Singapore, and Myanmar, inherited and maintained colonial laws that criminalized same-sex relations. In Malaysia, several authoritarian enclaves exist within one another. Apart from federal laws applicable to the entire population, some

[31] Boellstorff, 'The Emergence of Political Homophobia in Indonesia: Masculinity and National Belonging', in D. A. B. Murray (ed.), *Homophobias: Lust and Loathing Across Time and Space* (2009) 123; specifically on Myanmar, see Chua, 'Negotiating Social Norms' (n. 4).

[32] E.g. Carroll and Mendos (n. 6).

[33] E.g. Chua, *The Politics of Love* (n. 4).

[34] Seventy-two countries still outlaw same-sex relations: A. Gupta, *This Alien Legacy: The Origins of 'Sodomy' Laws in British Colonialism* (2008), www.hrw.org/report/2008/12/17/alien-legacy/origins-sodomy-laws-british-colonialism (last visited 22 February 2020).

[35] Human Rights Watch, 'No Support: Russia's "Gay Propaganda" Law Imperils LGBT Youth' (2018), https://www.hrw.org/report/2018/12/11/no-support/russias-gay-propaganda-law-imperils-lgbt-youth (last visited 22 February 2020).

Malaysian states have enacted Shariah laws outlawing homosexual relations between Muslim men or women.[36]

Legal oppression could also come from the enforcement of proxy laws, which are laws not explicitly worded against conduct or identities associated with sexual and gender minorities but are deployed selectively against this population. For example, in Singapore, the police used to raid gay businesses on the pretext of noise violations, or entrap gay men and arrest them for molestation, that is, 'outraging the modesty' of the undercover officer.[37] In Myanmar, police officers usually do not cite the anti-sodomy law, but rely on general provisions that empower police to arrest anybody whom they deem to be suspicious-looking in public after dark.[38] Local authorities in China, a country that does not directly penalize same-sex relations, was known for harassing and persecuting gay men on grounds of public order or safety,[39] as do Mexican and Brazilian police who take advantage of laws governing 'morality' or 'decency'.[40]

Then there are authoritarian enclaves of families, clans, and workplaces, where sexual and gender minorities conceal who they are out of concern that they might be socially sanctioned. Furthermore, these social institutions often contain subtle, indirect controls that rely on 'inner feelings of guilt and submission' to 'subordinate the person to the demands of the social order'.[41] A marginalized individual or group may regard their experiences as unproblematic or irrelevant to rights violations, such that mobilizing for their rights is not a consideration at all. A gay or transgender person may believe that they are committing a sin and not recognize their sense of shame and guilt as the result of layers of authoritarianism—state and religion—intertwined and imposed on them. For instance, according to popular beliefs in Burmese society, transgender women are people who accumulated bad karma in past lives, and have to suffer in this lifetime, the consequences of being transgender, a lowly social position. Hence, I found out in my study that Burmese transgender women often developed an inferior sense of self and did not imagine that they could or should try to change their structural conditions.[42]

4. Authoritarianism and Tactics of LGBTQ Rights Mobilization

Authoritarian conditions can be so oppressive that nobody wants to or can attempt to change them, but they are not necessarily determinative of rights mobilization. Subjective conditions, how people interpret and decide to respond to structural conditions, matter as well. Therefore, when LGBTQ rights mobilization does emerge in

[36] Muhammed and Amuda, 'LGBT: An Evaluation of Shariah Provisions and the Laws of Malaysia and Nigeria', 8 *Global Journal Al-Thaqafah* (2018) 15.

[37] Chua, *Mobilizing Gay Singapore* (n. 3).

[38] Chua and Gilbert, 'Sexual Orientation and Gender Minorities in Transition: LGBT Rights and Activism in Myanmar', 37 *HRQ* (2015) 1–28.

[39] Chua and Hildebrandt (n. 25).

[40] R. Dehesa, *Queering the Public Sphere in Mexico and Brazil: Sexual Rights Movements in Emerging Democracies* (2010).

[41] P. Nonet and P. Selznick, *Law and Society in Transition: Toward Responsive Law* (1978) 49–50.

[42] Chua, *The Politics of Love* (n. 4).

face of or despite authoritarian conditions, its manifestations—as strategies and tactics—are also the result of interactions between structural and subjective conditions.

For ease of discussion, I have divided strategies and tactics into two types, corresponding to authoritarian conditions directed at sexual and gender minorities, and to conditions that constrain rights mobilization. However, to be clear, the two types of strategies and tactics are not easy to distinguish, and the same course of action often embodies dual purposes. Both types can take the form of non-formal actions, which do not target formal state institutions, or formal actions, which aim at the courts, legislature, or administrative branches of government. Non-formal and formal actions are often implemented as part of multidimensional advocacy campaigns, and are not mutually exclusive of one another.[43]

A. Addressing Authoritarian LGBTQ Conditions

The non-formal actions of recruitment, community organizing, and consciousness raising try to encourage a population of sexual and gender minorities to recognize their grievances in terms of rights, speak up, and join collective action. These grassroots activities are directed at overcoming subtle authoritarian controls that prevent this population from framing their problems as rights, attributing blame to others, or seeking redress. LGBTQ rights activists carry out such activities in authoritarian enclaves for sexual and gender minorities in societies ruled by authoritarian and liberal governments alike. For example, although the homophile movement of the 1950s and 1960s in the US did not achieve social change—unlike its successor, the gay liberation movement—it helped some gay men and lesbians perceive themselves as members of an oppressed minority who share an identity subjected to systematic injustice.[44] In my study on Burmese LGBTQ rights activism, newcomers to the movement were largely ignorant of human rights or fearful of getting involved with a human rights–based movement. Blending human rights with local discourses about karma and self-responsibility, activists reframed police abuse, social ostracism, and discrimination as rights violations, educated newcomers that they are worthy of human rights, and encouraged them to participate in the movement.[45]

Demonstrations are also a non-formal tactic that challenges authoritarian conditions against sexual and gender minorities. In some cases, demonstrators protest a court ruling or legal prohibition against same-sex relations or marriage. Or, they march in pride parades to resist the hegemonic controls of sexuality, gender, and patriarchy. Walking together and expressing their sexual or gender identity openly is a show against inner feelings of guilt and shame, and a political act of building

[43] Cummings and NeJaime, 'Lawyering for Marriage Equality', 57 *UCLA Law Review* (2010) 1235.

[44] J. D'Emilio, *Sexual Politics, Sexual Communities* (2nd ed., 1998).

[45] Chua, *The Politics of Love* (n. 4). More generally on collective action framing, see Benford and Snow, 'Framing Processes and Social Movements: An Overview and Assessment', 26 *ARS* (2000) 611; Snow and Benford, 'Ideology, Frame Resonance, and Participant Mobilization', in Klandermans *et al.* (eds), *International Social Movement Research* (1988) 197. Generally, on how human rights are translated into local contexts, see S. E. Merry, *Human Rights and Gender Violence: Translating International Law into Local Justice* (2006); on LGBTQ rights, see Chua, 'Vernacular Mobilization' (n. 4).

collective identity. Nowadays pride parades take place in major cities around the world, including Mexico City, New York City, Taipei, Seoul, Shanghai, Sydney, Hanoi, Colombo, Johannesburg, and London.

In Singapore, however, LGBTQ rights activists do not hold pride parades but an annual alternative called Pink Dot in a park where the government allows public assembly without prior licensing approval.[46] On Pink Dot day, participants dress in pink attire and go to this public park, picnic together, watch musical performances, and then form a pink human dot in the centre of the park. Pink Dot activists capture the formation with aerial photography and videos, and circulate them online. Since its inception in 2009 with 2,000 participants, Pink Dot has grown to over 20,000 participants. Its activists want to show that support for sexual and gender minorities is widespread among the general population. In the past five years, they even openly appealed to the government to repeal the law that criminalizes consensual same-sex relations. As to why these Singaporean activists created Pink Dot instead of organizing a pride parade is a question of dealing with the structural constraints on rights activism, which I examine in the next subsection.

Among formal tactics challenging authoritarian LGBTQ conditions, litigation is probably the most well known. Individuals and LGBTQ rights groups sue in court for legal reform of LGBTQ authoritarian enclaves within authoritarian as well as liberal states. Their court cases challenge criminalization, non-legal recognition of same-sex unions, and other discriminatory practices in national regimes, subnational governments, and municipalities. They take place in domestic courts as wide-ranging as South Africa,[47] Singapore,[48] Hong Kong,[49] Taiwan,[50] United States,[51] and India,[52] and supranational bodies such as the Inter-American Commission on Human Rights,[53] European Court of Human Rights,[54] and United Nations Human Rights Committee.[55] Even if they doubt their prospects of winning, LGBTQ rights advocates push forward with litigation, hoping at least to gain publicity, bring attention to their cause, expose state failures, and rally support.[56]

Besides the courts, activists lobby the legislature to amend or enact laws, write complaint letters, or apply international pressure on the executive. In Japan, whereas some groups called on their national government to recognize same-sex unions so that it

[46] However, speakers are required to register in advance with the police and to abide by preset conditions, such as avoid talking about issues about race or religion that the state deems to be sensitive: Chua, *Mobilizing Gay Singapore* (n. 3) 80.

[47] E.g. *The National Coalition for Gay and Lesbian Equality v. The Minister of Justice* (ZACC 15, 1999 (1) SA 6 (CC), 1998 (12) BCLR 1517 (CC).

[48] E.g. *Lim Meng Suang and Kenneth Chee Mun-Leong v. Attorney-General* [2015] 1 Singapore Law Reports 26.

[49] E.g. *W. v. Registrar of Marriages* [2013] Hong Kong Court of Final Appeal 39.

[50] E.g. J.Y. Interpretation No. 748 (2017).

[51] E.g. E. A. Andersen, *Out of the Closets and into the Courts: Legal Opportunity Structure and Gay Rights Litigation* (2005); NeJaime, 'The Legal Mobilization Dilemma', 61 *Emory Law Journal* (2012) 663.

[52] E.g. *Navtej Singh Johar v. Union of India* (Writ Petition Criminal) No. 76 of 2016 (S.C.).

[53] E.g. C. Mounsey, 'Govt Given Three Months to Answer Challenge to Anti-Same Sex Laws', *Barbados Today* (27 July 2019), https://barbadostoday.bb/2019/07/27/govt-given-three-months-to-answer-challenge-to-anti-same-sex-laws/ (last visited 22 February 2020).

[54] E.g. *Dudgeon v. United Kingdom,* [1981] 4 EHRR 149, [1981] ECHR 5.

[55] E.g. *Toonen v. Australia*, Communication No. 488/1992, UN Doc CCPR/C/50/D/488/1992 (1994).

[56] E.g. Chua, 'Collective Litigation' (n. 3).

could catch up with other developed nations, other activists persuaded municipal governments to allow same-sex couples to register their partnerships at ward offices.[57] In 2009, when the Singaporean government conducted a comprehensive review of the Penal Code, LGBTQ rights activists collected signatures and petitioned the legislature to repeal the provision that criminalized same-sex relations.[58] During earlier days of their movement, patrons of a gay bar submitted a letter to the Singaporean police commissioner complaining about the conduct of officers who raided the bar and detained them overnight.

B. Addressing Authoritarian Constraints on Rights Mobilization

More often than not, LGBTQ rights activists do not carry out strategies and tactics with the sole purpose of overcoming, defeating, or circumventing authoritarian conditions that restrict their freedoms to mobilize. Usually, they deal with authoritarian constraints on rights mobilization in tandem with making claims for LGBTQ rights. On other occasions, they carry out tactics that embody both purposes of addressing these general constraints and claiming LGBTQ rights.

When recruiting participants, carrying out consciousness-raising work, or building community at the grassroots, LGBTQ rights activists—especially those in authoritarian states—also have to find ways to hold meetings and workshops without being raided or shut down by authorities. For example, during the early days of the Burmese LGBTQ rights movement, leaders based their headquarters in neighbouring Thailand to evade surveillance and clamp down. They used their underground network to recruit and vet new participants in Myanmar. Surreptitiously, they invited people who were trustworthy and courageous enough to navigate state restrictions on freedom of movement to travel to Thailand, partake in their activities, and then return home to start grassroots organizing in their hometowns.

To hold demonstrations, activists also have to consider the safety of participants and make plans with public assembly regulations in mind, whether it is to obey or flout them. In Singapore, the Pink Dot alternative to the pride parade aptly illustrates how activists simultaneously asserted LGBTQ rights and demonstrated publicly despite the restrictions on civil–political liberties. By staying within the park where the government has pre-authorized assembly and speech, Pink Dot's organizers obeyed state law and thus earned political legitimacy. At the same time, they pushed Singapore's political norms against confrontation. Before Pink Dot, no activist would have organized a public gathering of sexual and gender minorities. Pink Dot organizers not only assembled thousands of people in a public space, but also took advantage of online video and photographs to break the confines of that physical space.[59]

[57] Khor *et al.*, 'Global Norms, State Regulations, and Local Activism Marriage Equality and Same-Sex Partnership, Sexual Orientation, and Gender Identity Rights in Japan and Hong Kong', in Bosia *et al.* (eds), *The Oxford Handbook of Global LGBT and Sexual Diversity Politics* (2018; Tang *et al.*, 'Legal Recognition of Same-Sex Partnerships: A Comparative Study of Hong Kong, Taiwan and Japan', 68 *The Sociological Review* (2020) 192.

[58] Chua, 'Rights Mobilization' (n. 3).

[59] Chua, 'Pragmatic Resistance' (n. 3); Chua, *Mobilizing Gay Singapore* (n. 3).

When it comes to formal tactics, although LGBTQ rights activists typically litigate, lobby, or petition state actors to fight *for* LGBTQ rights, occasionally they do so to fend off authoritarian constraints on rights mobilization. Thus, formal tactics of LGBTQ rights can be part of a defensive strategy, rather than an offensive manoeuvre. For example, in 2011, the Malaysian police banned the sexuality rights festival known as Seksualiti Merdeka on grounds of public order. The festival, an annual event held in the Malaysian capital city, features workshops, stage performances, art, film screenings, and talks. LGBTQ rights leaders of the festival filed a judicial review of the police ban, though they ultimately failed to convince the High Court to rule in their favour. [60]

5. Authoritarianism and Implications of LGBTQ Rights Mobilization

The consequences of LGBTQ rights mobilization, particularly its prospects for social change, have been hotly debated. The answers often have much to do with the professional background of the critic or proponent, for instance, scholar, practitioner, or activist, and their theoretical orientation and disciplinary training. As a sociolegal scholar who has conducted fieldwork on LGBTQ rights mobilization and spoken to hundreds of activists, I emphasize grounding any assessment of mobilization outcomes in the empirical realities of research subjects and sites: the interactions between structural conditions, particularly the nature of authoritarianism, and the subjective conditions of social actors involved in LGBTQ rights mobilization. The interactions give rise to ongoing political processes in which outcomes that alter structural or subjective conditions go on to influence subsequent interactions and effects of LGBTQ rights mobilization.

When assessing these outcomes, it is critical to consider the achievements of tactics that address authoritarian conditions targeted at sexual and gender minorities, as well as the accomplishment of tactics aimed at overcoming authoritarian controls on rights mobilization. It is also important to pay attention to diverse types of tactics, those taking centre stage in formal state institutions, and those far away from them at the grassroots and on the streets. Some of these tactics successfully make use of the instrumental power of rights, whereas others harness the connotative power of rights, or both.

A. Gains from LGBTQ Rights Mobilization

Successful LGBTQ rights mobilization can produce instrumental effects by removing the direct controls imposed on sexual and gender minorities. Decriminalization reduces dangers and threats of blackmail and persecution. Anti-discrimination laws, such as constitutional provisions that prohibit discrimination against 'sexual

[60] Lee, 'Sexuality Rights Activism in Malaysia: The Case of Seksualiti Merdeka', in M. Ford (ed.), *Social Activism in Southeast Asia* (2013) 170.

minorities' (e.g. Nepal) or on the basis of 'sexual orientation' (e.g. South Africa), civil rights legislation, and hate crime laws,[61] provide legal avenues for sexual and gender minorities to expose and sanction unequal treatment and abuse. And legal recognition of same-sex families and gender identities opens up access to public benefits, services, and facilities.

An instrumental gain could catalyse further mobilization, energizing more activists to claim for LGBTQ rights, thus tapping into the connotative power of rights. For example, after the Indian Supreme Court struck down its anti-sodomy law, Section 377 of the Penal Code, the decision, and widespread celebration in India inspired Singaporean LGBTQ rights activists. Within weeks, they organized a fresh round of petitions to the government to reconsider their own penal law against consensual same-sex relations. Shortly afterwards, a few individuals stepped forward to file new lawsuits that once again challenged the penal law's constitutionality.[62]

LGBTQ rights activists can also benefit from the connotative power of rights without achieving any instrumental gain with formal tactics. As part of grassroots tactics, by strategically framing their issues as rights violations, they often can create resonance for their claims and obtain assistance from transnational human rights groups and foreign governments.[63] For instance, during its formative years in Thailand, Myanmar's LGBTQ rights movement received European funding for human rights training workshops and other rights-themed events. Movement leaders recruited and brought new participants from Myanmar to Thailand to attend these events, where they learned about human rights and felt empowered to join the movement. By the time the movement's national organization relocated from Chiang Mai, Thailand, to Yangon in 2013, it had in place a network of grassroots organizers from dozens of locations, ready to carry out further recruitment, training, and advocacy work.

In addition, non-formal tactics can produce symbolic effects of rights that help overcome indirect and direct controls over time. Grassroots recruitment, community building, and consciousness-raising, which make up the creeping phase of collective mobilization,[64] shore up courage and experience to mount bolder claims against direct controls. For almost 20 years, Singapore's LGBTQ rights movement did not openly push for legal reform or formal recognition of any LGBTQ right. These activists, nevertheless, found inspiration in rights to affirm the dignity and equality of sexual and gender minorities. They provided support to those struggling with their identities, and quietly cultivated a community that grew in size and diversity of groups. Gradually, these groups engaged the media and state openly as LGBTQ rights activists. The community support and courage to come out as LGBTQ rights activists thus enabled them in later years to organize a litigation campaign for decriminalization.[65]

Grassroots efforts can also lay the foundation for overcoming elusive controls that foster shame and fear of being known as a gay man, lesbian, transgender person, or

[61] E.g. Canada, El Salvador, and New Zealand have enacted hate crime laws: Carroll and Mendos (n. 6).

[62] Chua (n. 6).

[63] Thoreson, 'Queering Human Rights: The Yogyakarta Principles and the Norm that Dare Not Speak Its Name', 8 *Journal of Human Rights* (2009) 323–339; Thoreson, 'Realizing Rights in Manila: Brokers and the Mediation of Sexual Politics in the Philippines', 18 *GLQ* (2012) 529.

[64] D'Emilio (n. 44) 251–262.

[65] Chua, 'Pragmatic Resistance' (n. 3); Chua, *Mobilizing Gay Singapore* (n. 3).

rights activist. In Singapore, LGBTQ rights activists used rights to help sexual and gender minorities rethink taken-for-granted assumptions, and recalibrate what is appropriate or inappropriate. In my study on Myanmar, changes to one's sense of self—as beings worthy of human rights—too, increased the LGBTQ rights movement's organizational capacity. The movement's rights-themed workshops and events attempt to alter the way sexual and gender minorities understand their social positions, relationships, and responsibility, motivate them to join the movement, and take up a new collective identity known as LGBTQ rights activists. This group of people became a new political claimant, a community who represents and seeks rights recognition for a minority population hitherto missing from Burmese rights politics.[66]

By and large, the tactics of LGBTQ rights mobilization, whether targeted at changing authoritarian LGBTQ conditions or constraints on rights activism, are meant to achieve the former. Nonetheless, it may be possible for either type of tactics to loosen the controls on rights mobilization generally, especially in authoritarian states. One speculation that I have is Pink Dot in Singapore. Pink Dot activists creatively made use of what was once a space where only the lone opposition politician would occasionally stand and speak with a loud hailer, trying to catch the attention of passers-by. In the past 10 years since the inception of Pink Dot, liberal and conservatives alike have held a number of demonstrations at the park. The most recent was the 2019 climate change rally. About 2,000 people attended the event organized by Singaporean youth in solidarity with the global youth climate movement.[67] Of course, it is difficult to draw causal links between Pink Dot and the rise in popularity of public assemblies. Perhaps Pink Dot is part of the trend among Singaporeans to slowly expand the constraints on rights mobilization. But it is nevertheless worthwhile to look out for such possible changes in the societies where scholars conduct research on LGBTQ rights mobilization.

B. Critiques of LGBTQ Rights Mobilization

In spite of its many benefits, sociolegal scholars and other researchers have questioned rights mobilization as a strategy against the authoritarian conditions of sexual and gender minorities. The doubts and criticisms are an extension and variation of the debates about the effectiveness and efficacy of rights in achieving social change more generally. For LGBTQ rights, the debate is usually linked to contestations over the development of human rights after the Second World War, one that intensified as human rights were explicitly extended to sexuality and gender identity after the early 1990s.[68]

The criticisms about the ineffectual, even harmful, nature of rights, are wide-ranging. Published in volumes of articles and books, they come from sociolegal scholars,

[66] Chua, *The Politics of Love* (n. 4).

[67] Low and Elangovan, 'Youths as Young as 11 Lead the Way for Singapore's Inaugural Climate Rally', *Today* (22 Sept. 2019), https://www.todayonline.com/singapore/youths-young-11-lead-way-singapores-inaugural-climate-rally (last visited 23 February 2020).

[68] See n. 6.

critical legal scholars, and many more. Some of the common criticisms as applied to LGBTQ rights are considered in the next paragraphs.

Sexual and gender minorities around the world remain largely unprotected from the harms and violations from which rights are supposed to shield them. In some instances, their rights are recognized on the books, in court opinions, statutes, and ordinances, but opponents find ways to work around them. For example, a clerk may refuse to issue marriage licences to gay couples.[69] Laws and court judgments are not self-enforcing, and rely on activists or individuals willing to confront non-abiding conduct. My earlier concerns about how authoritarianism obstructs LGBTQ rights mobilization—by weakening the desire or capacity to assert rights claims—come to the fore once more. In other instances, LGBTQ rights are not even protected on the books. There, LGBTQ rights activists could run into the lack of cultural resonance or political legitimacy for rights. If they employ rights tactics, they could be accused of promoting undesirable Western culture and heighten backlash from the state and other opponents, thus worsening local conditions.[70]

Moreover, the use of Western funding or assistance could reinforce an unequal distribution of power. Typically, such funds go to organizations able and willing to embrace rights discourse. In Myanmar, LGBTQ rights activists from the movement's national organization control the funding from international organizations and set the agenda for their grassroots counterparts. Hence, critics argue that rights, embodying Western discourses of moral individualism, gets privileged at the expense of alternative solutions based on local discourses.[71] In the Global North, this kind of criticism is associated with charges about deradicalization[72] or the mainstreaming effects of rights;[73] that is, rights mobilization, for such laws as same-sex marriage, redirects and reshapes activists' goals from culturally transformative aspirations and radical tactics to conservative reforms to patriarchal, heterosexist institutions. In the Global South, critics additionally argue that rights mobilization imports the identities of 'LGBTQ' into the local context, and risks supplanting subjectivities of sexuality and gender of local origins.[74]

Indeed, LGBTQ rights mobilization does not always achieve its intended purposes, and rights discourse can be ineffectual or wield undue hegemonic influence. On the other hand, they can also be beneficial and helpful to sexual and gender minorities. For activists who are situated in less authoritarian states but contend with authoritarian enclaves for sexual and gender minorities, perhaps rights mobilization is a politically

[69] E.g. Stempel, 'Kentucky Clerk Who Refused Same-Sex Marriage Licenses Can Be Sued', *Reuters* (24 Aug. 2019), https://www.reuters.com/article/us-usa-kentucky-weddings/kentucky-clerk-who-refused-same-sex-marriage-licenses-can-be-sued-idUSKCN1VD284 (last visited 22 February 2020).

[70] E.g. Massad, 'Re-orienting Desire: The Gay International and the Arab World', 14 *Public Culture* (2002) 361; Currier (n. 19); Boyd, 'The Problem with Freedom: Homosexuality and Human Rights in Uganda', 86 *Anthropological Quarterly* (2013) 697.

[71] Thoreson, 'LGBT human rights in the Age of Human Rights', 14 *Scholar & Feminist Online* (2017), http://sfonline.barnard.edu/thinking-queer-activism-transnationally/lgbt-human-rights-in-the-age-of-human-rights/ (last visited 23 February 2020).

[72] Albiston, 'The Dark Side of Litigation as a Social Movement Strategy' 96 *Iowa Law Review Bulletin* 61; Leachman, 'From Protest to Perry: How Litigation Shaped the LGBT Movement's Agenda', 47 *UC Davis Law Review* (2014) 1667.

[73] U. Vaid, *Virtual Equality: The Mainstreaming of Gay and Lesbian Liberation* (1995).

[74] E.g. Massad (n. 70).

legitimate strategy, and LGBTQ rights claims fit into a familiar cultural discourse. The same cannot be said of those struggling in authoritarian enclaves within authoritarian regimes where rights mobilization generally is much more repressed, even dangerous. Under such circumstances, rights may be liberating to the people learning to assert them, and transgressive in the eyes of the powerful in charge.[75] They could undermine deeply rooted beliefs that sustain social hierarchy and reduce the suffering inflicted by authoritarianism. To the critical outsider observing from where rights are part of politics as usual, rights may seem narrow and unimaginative. But for activists fighting on the ground, in Singapore, Myanmar, and many more places where layers of authoritarianism imbricate, perhaps they worry less about the debates over reinforcing rights hegemony, when their hegemony is the deprivation of rights.[76]

In short, when taking a sociolegal approach to studying the effects of LGBTQ rights, the criticisms and pitfalls of rights may or may not apply to an authoritarian regime in question. With this approach, it is important not to adopt entrenched normative positions[77] or succumb to intellectual blackmail[78] over the position one ought to take for or against LGBTQ rights. I hope that scholars will consider adopting my proposed approach in this chapter: understand LGBTQ rights mobilization through the interactions between structural conditions and the subjectivities of the people who live, experience, and act under those conditions.

6. Conclusion

In this chapter, I introduced two ideas about LGBTQ rights mobilization and its relationship to authoritarianism. The first idea is that 'authoritarianism is all over'. Layers of authoritarianism coexist, taking the shape of authoritarian states and enclaves. The second idea is that LGBTQ rights emerge from mobilization, a series of political processes through which social actors interpret their encounters with structural conditions, and tailor their responses according to who they are, including whether or not to refer to rights.

Both ideas underscore authoritarianism and LGBTQ rights as social phenomena. The features of authoritarianism and LGBTQ rights vary across political, social, and legal contexts. What those features look like and how they vary would emerge from the data and data analysis of sociolegal inquiry.

Therefore, the perspective that 'authoritarianism is all over' allows us to see how authoritarianism distinctively affects sexual and gender minorities in each context. At the same time, it helps us recognize that most sexual and gender minorities around the

[75] Whether rights mobilization is radical or resonant depends on the context and culture: Ferree, 'Resonance and Radicalism: Feminist Framing in the Abortion Debates of the United States and Germany', 109 *American Journal of Sociology* (2003) 304.

[76] In response to scholars who criticize the use of such terms as 'gay' and 'lesbian' in India, Ruth Vanita writes, 'It is significant that it is usually those who have already obtained most of their basic civil rights and liberties in first-world environments who object to the use of these terms in third-world contexts': 'Introduction', in R. Vanita (ed.), *Queering India* (2002) 1, at 5.

[77] McCann, 'Law and Social Movements: Contemporary Perspectives' 2 *ARLSS* (2006) 17.

[78] F. Kurasawa, *The Work of Global Justice: Human Rights as Practice* (2007) 200.

world still live under some degree of oppression, and allows us to appreciate connections between LGBTQ rights mobilization in authoritarian states and in authoritarian enclaves within more liberal-democratic states. Yet, focusing on mobilization on the ground, we become keenly aware that the relationship between LGBTQ rights mobilization and authoritarianism is contingent, as are the implications of LGBTQ rights. We find hope that authoritarianism alone does not determine the development of LGBTQ rights mobilization, even though harsh and cruel conditions can be highly influential. Human agency plays an important part, too. Sometimes, sexual and gender minorities lump their problems, accepting or resigning themselves to their unhappy circumstances. Other times, they assert their rights, even become activists, inspired by friends and leaders, or impelled by repression. And, instead of insistently defending or criticizing LGBTQ rights, we find ease with and revelation in uncertainties, which are often the empirical realities of those who struggle under authoritarianism.

3

Women, Peace, and Security

A Human Rights Agenda?

Christine Chinkin[*]

1. Introduction

What has become known as the Women, Peace and Security (WPS) agenda emanates from the ground-breaking Resolution 1325 adopted by the UN Security Council in October 2000. Resolution 1325 centres upon bringing women's experiences of armed conflict into decision-making and policy-making as an essential ingredient in the maintenance of international peace and security. It identifies three elements that can make a significant contribution to this primary responsibility of the Council:[1] (i) 'an understanding of the impact of armed conflict on women and girls'; (ii) 'effective institutional arrangements to guarantee their protection'; and (iii) 'full participation in the peace process'.[2] By May 2021, Resolution 1325 had been followed by nine other resolutions.[3] Taken together they accumulate a body of global normative standards and measures that are urged upon states, UN institutions, and civil society. WPS is accordingly appropriately called an agenda. But is it an international human rights agenda? In 2015 a Security Council commissioned *Global Study on the Implementation of Resolution 1325* stated that it had been 'conceived of and lobbied for as a human rights resolution that would promote the rights of women in conflict situations'.[4] This assertion sits somewhat strangely with its location in the Security Council rather than in the UN human rights institutions, a view that is reinforced by the comparatively widespread discussion of WPS in international relations and political science literature in contrast to that in international law or human rights.

The subject of this chapter is to ask whether WPS does have a place in a course and book on mobilizing human rights. The chapter first describes the evolution of WPS, focusing on its antecedents within women's social movements. It then examines the first two WPS resolutions, 1325 (2000) and 1820 (2008) in some detail and the subsequent resolutions more generally to determine the extent to which they

* This chapter is part of a project entitled 'A Gendered Peace' that has received funding from the European Research Council (ERC) as an Advanced Project under the European Union's Horizon 2020 research and innovation programme.

1 Art. 24 Charter of the United Nations, 1945.

2 Preamble SC Res. 1325 (2000).

3 SC Res. 1820 (2008); SC Res. 1888 (2009); SC Res. 1889 (2009); SC Res. 1960 (2010); SC Res. 2106 (2013); SC Res. 2122 (2013); SC Res. 2242 (2015); SC Res. 2467 (2019); SC Res. 2493 (2019).

4 R. Coomaraswamy *et al.*, *Preventing Conflict, Transforming Justice, Securing the Peace—A Global Study on the Implementation of Security Council Resolution 1325* (2015) 15 (hereinafter *Global Study*).

Christine Chinkin, *Women, Peace, and Security* In: *Legal Mobilization for Human Rights.* Edited by: Gráinne de Búrca, Oxford University Press. © Gráinne de Búrca and Christine Chinkin, 2022. DOI: 10.1093/oso/9780192866578.003.0003

can be understood as human rights instruments. The Security Council's approach to taking account of women's experiences in conflict is contrasted with that of the Committee on Elimination of Discrimination against Women (CEDAW Committee) in its General Recommendation No. 30 on Women in Conflict Prevention, Conflict and Post-Conflict Situations,[5] adopted on the same day as WPS Resolution 2122—18 October 2013. Up until 2015 the WPS resolutions were adopted unanimously, and their content was largely uncontroversial. The changed political environment in 2019 meant that the negotiation of Resolution 2467 in April 2019 was strongly contested around issues relating to women's sexual and reproductive rights and understandings of gender. This resolution is therefore considered in more detail. The chapter also considers the extent to which WPS cuts across the UN institutional divide between human rights (Geneva) and security (New York/Security Council). It concludes that women's mobilization today around the WPS agenda is not so much about advancement of women's rights as about retaining the headway made in Resolution 1325.

A. The Origins of WPS: Women's Mobilization around Peace and Human Rights

The preamble to Resolution 1325 recognizes the commitments made in the 1995 Beijing Declaration and Platform for Action that constitute a blueprint for women's advancement and which for many remain the high spot of achievement by women's organizations.[6] But it is silent about what by 1995 had become a long history of lobbying and campaigning for women's political and participatory rights, rights for working women, for world peace, and universal disarmament. A key moment for urging peace was the Women's International Congress that met in the Hague in 1915. This was a coming together of women from across Europe and the United States in the midst of World War I to protest the 'madness and horror of war',[7] demand an institutional framework for peace in which women could participate alongside men[8] and advocate for international cooperation and universal disarmament.[9] They resolved to meet again at the termination of the war, which they did four years later in Zurich. There, their understanding of what was needed for peace led the delegates to reject the Versailles Treaty[10] and to urge the inclusion of a Women's Charter in the Peace Treaty. The lengthy Women's Charter asserts the 'social, political and economic status of women' to be a matter of 'supreme international importance'. Much of it is cast in

[5] CEDAW/C/ GC/30, 2013.

[6] Preamble SC Res. 1325 also recalls the Outcome document of the twenty-third Special Session of the United Nations General Assembly, Women 2000: Gender Equality, Development and Peace for the Twenty-First Century, A/S-23/10/Rev.1, 2000.

[7] International Congress of Women, The Hague, 28 April–1 May 1915, Resolution I at http://www2.ub.gu.se/kvinndata/portaler/fred/samarbete/pdf/resolutions_1915.pdf.

[8] Ibid. Resolution 3: 'That women should be granted equal political rights with men'.

[9] Ibid. Resolution 12.

[10] Women's International League for Peace and Freedom, 2nd Congress, Zurich, Switzerland, 1919, Resolution II: 'This International Congress of Women expresses its deep regret that the terms of peace proposed at Versailles should so seriously violate the principles upon which alone a just and lasting peace can be secured', https://wilpf.org/wp-content/uploads/2012/08/WILPF_triennial_congress_1919.pdf.

the language of rights, including personal, civil, and participatory rights as well as 'the same pay as men for the same work'. The proposed Women's Charter brought together demands for what we now call women's human rights with those for peace in a post-conflict context. Admittedly it was an agenda for white women; the sole Black woman delegate, Mary Church Terrell, demanded of a Congress plenary that it accept that an understanding of peace necessitates consideration of race.[11]

Some 70 years later, in the 1990s, women mobilized around these same issues at the global summit meetings of the decade. At the Vienna World Conference on Human Rights in 1993 women's non-governmental organizations (NGOs) gained some key advances in the final documents: that the human rights of women and of the girl-child are an inalienable, integral, and indivisible part of universal human rights and that women's rights are human rights.[12] Specific attention turned to the elimination of what had been defined the previous year as 'gender-based violence'[13] in public and private life. The Vienna summit was held while the war in Bosnia was taking place just a short distance away with the shocking revelations of the sexual violence occurring within it that could not be ignored. Challenging the traditional binary divide between international humanitarian law (IHL) as applicable to international or non-international armed conflict and international human rights law to peacetime, the Conference declared that 'violations of the human rights of women in situations of armed conflict are violations of the fundamental principles of international human rights and humanitarian law, requiring ... a particularly effective response'.[14] This conveyed the germ of understanding of a continuum of gender-based violence against women: that conflict exacerbates women's pre-existing inequalities and their experience of violence committed because they are women in non-conflict situations rather than understanding such violence in conflict situations as constituting something entirely different in kind. Vienna also articulated mainstreaming as a tool for the advancement of women's human rights.[15]

Two years later, at the Fourth World Conference on Women in Beijing, these principles were amplified and fleshed out in the critical areas of concern relating to women and violence (critical area of concern D) and women and human rights (critical area of concern I).[16] Women's diversity was recognized,[17] as were the multiple factors that impede women's enjoyment of their rights including their race, age, language, ethnicity, culture, religion, disability, indigeneity, family, and socio-economic status; that they live in rural or isolated environments; are refugees, internally displaced, immigrants,

[11] M. Siegel, *Peace on Our Terms: The Global Battle for Women's Rights after the First World War* (2020) 80: 'A lasting peace is an impossibility as long as the colored races are subject to injustice'.

[12] UN General Assembly, Vienna Declaration and Programme of Action, 1993, A/CONF.157/23, I, para. 18; II, para. 38.

[13] Committee on the Elimination of Discrimination against Women, General Recommendation No. 19, Violence against Women, 11th session 1992, HRI/GEN/1/Rev.8, para. 6 defines gender-based violence as 'violence that is directed against a woman because she is a woman or that affects women disproportionately'.

[14] Vienna Declaration and Programme of Action (n. 12), para. II, 38.

[15] Ibid. para. II, 37.

[16] Beijing Declaration and Platform for Action, 1995, A/CONF.177/20 (1995) and A/CONF.177/20/Add.1 (1995) (hereinafter Beijing DPFA).

[17] The Convention on Elimination of All Forms of Discrimination against Women, 1979, 1249 UNTS 13 (CEDAW) had made little recognition of difference between women other than in Article 14 on rural women.

or migrant workers.[18] It was also acknowledged that many women are particularly affected by environmental disasters and infectious diseases. Women's sexuality however remained controversial and the rights of lesbian or trans women were not expressly included. Under the rubric of 'women and armed conflict', governments and international institutions were to '[i]ncrease the participation of women in conflict resolution at decision-making levels and protect women living in situations of armed and other conflicts or under foreign occupation'.[19] The Beijing Platform for Action noted women's leading role in the peace movement and governments were to work actively towards 'general and complete disarmament under strict and effective international control'.[20] In line with the Cairo Conference held a year earlier,[21] Beijing also spelled out that women's human rights include having control over and deciding freely and responsibly on matters related to their sexuality and their sexual and reproductive health, free from coercion, discrimination, and violence.[22]

Long-term and focused activism thus paid off in the articulation in the 1990s of key principles relating to women's human rights, eradication of gender-based violence against women, and protection of women in armed conflict that supplemented earlier normative instruments, in particular the Convention on the Elimination of All Forms of Discrimination against Women (CEDAW).[23] But there was a feeling of dismay when some two months after Beijing no local women participated in the Dayton peace process which brought an end to the armed conflict in Bosnia. Further, despite the widespread and highly publicized sexual violence in that conflict, there was little substantive reference to women's experiences in the lengthy peace agreement.[24] Attention then turned to bringing commitment to women's rights—especially with respect to women's participation and ending impunity for sexual violence in conflict—into a more politically powerful arena than the General Assembly and its global summit meetings. NGOs canvassed the Security Council, mobilizing global support through regional meetings, engaging like-minded states as champions, such as Namibia and Bangladesh from the Global South and the United Kingdom (then with a Labour government committed to an ethical foreign policy) from the Global North, and institutional support in the form of the Commission on the Status of Women, the Division for the Advancement of Women, and UNIFEM (the latter two now part of UN Women).[25] Civil society solidarity was strengthened by the creation of an NGO Working Group on Women and International Peace and Security.[26] Security Council

[18] Beijing DPFA, para. 46.

[19] Ibid., strategic objective E.1.

[20] Ibid., para. 28 and 143(f)(i).

[21] International Conference on Population and Development, Cairo, Egypt, September 1994, A/CONF.171/13/Rev.1.

[22] Beijing DPFA, para. 96.

[23] n. 17.

[24] General Framework Agreement for Peace for Bosnia and Herzegovina, Dayton, initialled 21 November 1995, signed Paris 14 December 1995.

[25] Anderlini, 'Civil Society's Leadership in Adopting 1325 Resolution', in S. E. Davies and J. True (eds), *Oxford Handbook of Women, Peace and Security* (2019) 38.

[26] Members of the NGO Working Group were International Alert, the Women's International League for Peace and Freedom, The Hague Appeal for Peace, the International Women's Tribunal Center, the Women's Caucus for Gender Justice and the Women's Commission for Refugee Women and Children; Hill *et al.*, 'Nongovernmental Organizations' Role in the Buildup and Implementation of Security Council Resolution 1325', 28 *Signs* (2003), 1255 at 1258.

members were lobbied in an Arria formula meeting outside the formal structures of debate and resolution negotiation. In 2000 this mobilization succeeded in the adoption of Resolution 1325.[27]

2. WPS: A Women's Human Rights Agenda?

A. The First WPS Resolutions

1. Resolution 1325 (2000)

Resolution 1325 was the outcome of a rich history of women's human rights and peace activism transported into the language of the Security Council. This first WPS resolution has three main themes: gender balance; integrating a gender perspective; and ending the impunity of perpetrators of sexual and other violence against women and girls in armed conflict. Gender balance is about numbers, increasing women's participation and representation in all decision-making levels in national, regional, and international institutions and mechanisms for the prevention, management, and resolution of conflict and ensuring more women in institutional positions such as special representatives and envoys in United Nations field-based operations. No reason for this objective is given and it is simply assumed that the involvement of women in processes for the prevention and resolution of conflict is important. Integrating a gender perspective is seeking to give effect to mainstreaming as extolled by the global summit meetings earlier in the decade. Resolution 1325 urges all actors involved to take a gender perspective in post-conflict policymaking, such as by supporting local women's peace initiatives and indigenous processes for conflict resolution and ensuring the protection of and respect for the human rights of women and girls, particularly as they relate to the constitution, the electoral system, the police and the judiciary—the core components of post-conflict constitution building.[28]

Resolution 1325 calls upon 'all parties to armed conflict' to 'respect' CEDAW and its Optional Protocol.[29] Parties to armed conflict include non-state actors such as armed militia that are not parties to CEDAW (or any other international treaty)[30] and the Council does not elucidate the legal basis for its application of treaties to them.[31] The incorporation of CEDAW into the operative paragraphs of Resolution 1325 is significant as it remains the principal instrument for the guarantee of women's human rights, legally binding on states parties.[32] The final documents of the global summit

[27] For contemporary issues addressed by the Security Council that complement Resolution 1325, see Chinkin, 'Adoption of 1325 Resolution', in Davies and True (n. 25) 26.

[28] SC Res. 1325 (2000) para. 8.

[29] Optional Protocol to the Convention on the Elimination of All Forms of Discrimination against Women, 1999, 2131 UNTS 83.

[30] Art. 2(1)(a) Vienna Convention on the Law of Treaties, 1969, 1155 UNTS 331.

[31] Nor does the Security Council reference the Deeds of Commitment prepared by Geneva Call through which armed groups commit to comply with principles of international law; e.g. Deed of Commitment under Geneva Call for the Prohibition of Sexual Violence in Situations of Armed Conflict and towards the Elimination of Gender Discrimination, https://www.genevacall.org/wp-content/uploads/2019/07/DoC-Prohibiting-sexual-violence-and-gender-discrimination.pdf.

[32] Resolution 1325 also calls upon states to respect the Convention on the Rights of the Child, 1989, 1577 UNTS 3, which is applicable to girls and boys under 18 years of age.

meetings are important as setting out political commitments and providing states and other actors with programmes for action but do not per se constitute formally legally binding instruments. They are a form of 'soft law' that may become legally binding through recognition as customary international law.[33] Nor is Resolution 1325 in legally binding form. It is a thematic resolution of the Security Council adopted under UN Charter chapter VI, recommendatory rather than deciding upon action and therefore not coming within the terms of Article 25 UN Charter.[34] Embedding WPS within the Security Council, accorded it political weight but did not confer legal status except to the extent that it incorporates already existing legal obligations. States parties to CEDAW and the Convention on the Rights of the Child (CRC) are already obliged to 'respect, protect and fulfil' the Conventions' provisions,[35] not merely to 'respect' them as called for by the Security Council.

Following the Beijing Platform for Action, Resolution 1325 makes women's participation and representation central. The first six paragraphs call for increased numbers of women across a range of decision-making functions before, during, and after conflict. CEDAW too addresses women's participation. Articles 7 and 8 require states parties to take appropriate measures to ensure women's equality with men with respect to political participation,[36] in representing their governments at the international level and in participation in the work of international organizations. In seeking only 'increased' and not 'equal' participation Resolution 1325 dilutes the international human rights standard set out in CEDAW. The CEDAW Committee has moreover asserted the elimination of discrimination against women to be an immediate obligation that must be carried out without delay.[37] This language is not repeated by the Security Council. Resolution 1325 urges women's 'full participation in the peace process' for its significant contribution 'to the maintenance and promotion of international peace and security'. Women's participation is thereby made pursuant to the Council's responsibility for security rather than to the enhancement of women's rights.

The Council addresses conflict-affected violence in two separate operative paragraphs. In paragraph 10 it calls upon all parties to armed conflict to protect women and girls from gender-based violence and in the following paragraph emphasizes the importance of ending impunity and of prosecution of those responsible for genocide, crimes against humanity, and war crimes including sexual and other violence against women and girls. The CEDAW Committee has explained that 'gender-based violence' is a form of discrimination within Article 1 CEDAW.[38] It has clarified states'

[33] C. Chinkin, *Women, Peace and Security and International Law* (2022), see chapter 2 for a detailed discussion of this point.

[34] Art. 25 Charter of the United Nations, 1945: 'The Members of the United Nations agree to accept and carry out the decisions of the Security Council in accordance with the present Charter'.

[35] CEDAW Committee, General Recommendation No. 28 on the Core Obligations of States Parties under Article 2 of the Convention on the Elimination of All Forms of Discrimination against Women, CEDAW/C/GC/28, 2010, para. 9: 'States parties must address all aspects of their legal obligations under the Convention to respect, protect and fulfil women's right to non-discrimination and to the enjoyment of equality'.

[36] This builds on the Convention on the Political Rights of Women, 1953, 193 UNTS 135.

[37] CEDAW Committee, General Recommendation No. 28 (n. 35) para. 29: 'The words "without delay" make it clear that the obligation of States parties to pursue their policy, by all appropriate means, is of an immediate nature'.

[38] CEDAW Committee, General Recommendation No. 19 (n. 13) para. 6: 'The definition of discrimination includes gender-based violence'.

obligations with respect to the acts of its own agents and their duty of due diligence to prevent, investigate and prosecute gender-based violence committed by non-state actors and to make reparation.[39] The Council's use of the expression 'gender-based violence' implies importation of this holistic human rights framework but the text of 1325 reduces state responsibility to protection. In paragraph 11 the language shifts to that of 'sexual violence', which unlike 'gender-based violence' has no accepted definition within human rights law. The focus is on individual criminal liability through prosecution, but without referring directly to IHL or international criminal law. Paragraph 9 does however call upon parties to conflict to 'respect' international law for the protection of civilians in armed conflict and to 'bear in mind' the Rome Statute of the International Criminal Court.

Is Resolution 1325 an instrument for advancing women's human rights in conflict settings as wished for by many of those who mobilized for its adoption? On the one hand, the resolution reaffirms the need to implement human rights law and states are explicitly reminded of relevant human rights instruments, CEDAW and CRC. On the other hand, concepts and obligations that were already part of human rights law are either unacknowledged or weakened. There is no provision for a monitoring body such as is provided for within the UN human rights treaties. Difficult questions of human rights law are evaded; for instance, the Council does not explore the human rights obligations of non-state actors but merely assumes the applicability of international law to them. But if Resolution 1325 is ambiguous as a human rights treaty the same is true of it as a feminist peace agenda, the objective of many feminist activists going back to the resolutions adopted at the Women's Congress in 1915 and the work of the Women's International League for Peace and Freedom (WILPF) since that time.[40] Despite lobbying by WILPF and relevant language in the Beijing Platform for Action, Resolution 1325 makes no mention of disarmament[41] (except in the narrow context of disarmament, demobilization, and reintegration (DDR)), reduction of military expenditure, or of any connection between promotion of women's human rights and peace, or between eradication of gender-based violence and sustainable peace.

2. Resolution 1820 (2008)

The next WPS resolution, 1820, was not adopted until eight years later in 2008 and the emphasis shifts from women's greater participation to protection of women and girls against sexual violence in armed conflict. Resolution 1820 stresses that sexual violence when used as a tactic of war can exacerbate armed conflict and may impede the restoration of international peace and security. Steps taken to prevent such sexual violence therefore contribute to the maintenance of international peace and security. The resolution demands that all parties to armed conflict immediately cease all acts of sexual violence against civilians and offers suggestions as to how women and girls can be protected against such violence.

[39] Ibid. See also CEDAW Committee, General Recommendation No. 35 on Gender-Based Violence against Women, Updating General Recommendation No. 19, CEDAW/C/GC/35, 2017.

[40] WILPF was created at The Hague in 1915 and is the oldest women's peace NGO.

[41] Preamble to CEDAW affirms that 'general and complete disarmament, in particular nuclear disarmament under strict and effective international control ... will promote social progress and development and as a consequence will contribute to the attainment of full equality between men and women'.

By emphasizing that sexual violence as a tactic of war is an impediment to international peace and security the Council rejects its characterization as an inevitable by-product of war and identifies it for what it is—a war crime, a crime against humanity, possibly genocidal, a crime of humiliation, and an assertion of power and control. It is of course also a violation of human rights, as had been spelled out in Vienna 15 years earlier, but this categorization is not repeated in Resolution 1820.

Under human rights law, all people are entitled to be free from sexual violence, not just civilians and not just women and girls.[42] The attention paid to sexual violence including rape as a tactic of war is limiting for women and girls within the civilian population at whom it is directed. It discounts the many other reasons for conflict-related sexual violence and that it is committed by the state as well as by a range of non-state actors. Nor does it take account of the additional vulnerabilities to gender-based discrimination and violence caused by factors such as displacement, collapse of social norms and structures, poverty, and unemployment. These contribute to further human rights violations against women and girls including the unavailability of appropriate healthcare following sexual violence and denial of their sexual and reproductive rights, harassment, lack of access to education, the destruction of shelter, livelihoods, and food for women who are the primary carers within their families and communities.[43] It has the potential to create a hierarchy of rights and of victims, contrary to the universalism of human rights. There is no direct reference to the Global South as the location of wartime sexual violence against civilians, but this is the tenor of the resolutions and is implied by the reference to the Council adopting measures to address widespread or systematic sexual violence when considering situations on its agenda—the majority of which are in the south. For WPS 'champions' such as the US[44] and UK, 'rapacious violence' happens in foreign territories, not at home.[45]

Human rights law has a lower explicit profile in Resolution 1820 than in Resolution 1325. CEDAW and CRC are confined to the preamble rather than integrated into the operative paragraphs. The general reaffirmation of states' obligations under IHL and international human rights law and of states' primary responsibility for protecting the human rights of their citizens and of individuals within their territory are also set out only in the preamble. The language of 'gender-based violence' (carrying with it the human rights framework for its elimination) is replaced by that of (all forms of) sexual violence with the emphasis on criminal prosecution and protection. Resolution 1820 assumes sexual violence committed by (male) military personnel[46] and women's security as both transgressed and upheld through military means.[47] In the Security Council's militarized and masculinized view of the world this inevitably involves the

[42] Men and boys as victims of conflict-affected sexual violence were not included in the WPS resolutions until the preamble SC Res. 2106 (2013) and then not again until SC Res. 2467 (2019) para. 28.

[43] E.g. Report of the detailed findings of the Group of Eminent International and Regional Experts on Yemen, *Situation of Human Rights in Yemen, Including Violations and Abuses Since September 2014*, A/HRC/42/CRP.1, 3 September 2019, paras 616–633.

[44] The US held the Presidency of the Security Council at the time of adoption of SC Res. 1820 (2008).

[45] Bourke, 'Reflections on Power: Discourses, Representations, Trauma', in G. Zipfel, R. Mühlhaüser, and K. Campbell (eds), *In Plain Sight: Sexual Violence in Armed Conflict* (2019) 93, at 96.

[46] SC Res. 1820, para. 3, includes military disciplinary measures, command responsibility, training troops, vetting of security forces and evacuation.

[47] E.g. SC Res. 1820, paras 6, 8, 9.

securitization of rights,[48] transforming people into objects of the security apparatus to be protected in the interests of international peace and security rather than as individual and collective rights bearers.

3. Security Council Resolutions on WPS: 2009–2015

By 2015 the WPS agenda was regularly framed around four so-called pillars: participation, protection against and prevention of conflict-affected sexual violence and relief and recovery. The six WPS resolutions adopted after Resolution 1820 and up to 2015 fluctuate between giving priority to women's participation in peacemaking and peacebuilding mechanisms and protecting women and girls from sexual violence in armed conflict with less attention given to prevention (including prevention of conflict) or relief and recovery. In 2015 there was a High-level Review of progress at the global, regional and national levels in implementing Resolution 1325[49] in light of the findings of the independent *Global Study*[50] and culminating in the adoption of Resolution 2242. The High-level Review debate was perhaps the apogee of enthusiasm for WPS: Resolution 2242 was sponsored by a record-breaking 75 states and there were 110 speakers during the two-day debate, the highest number in the Council's 70-year history. But human rights were spoken of in only 13 per cent of the speeches.[51] This section offers some reflections on WPS and human rights in the resolutions up to and including Resolution 2242. It considers that across the resolutions the message about human rights is ambivalent but that, overall, the human rights perspective in Resolution 1325—already weak—becomes further diluted. It offers five reasons for this conclusion.

First is the changed place of CEDAW and its Optional Protocol within the resolutions. Resolution 1325 had incorporated CEDAW into its operative paragraphs, but this does not occur again in the period to 2015. In some resolutions states' obligations under the Convention are recalled[52] or, in stronger language, reaffirmed,[53] but only within the preamble; in others CEDAW is omitted altogether.[54] The Security Council does urge non-party states to consider ratifying or acceding to the Convention but without the greater authority bestowed by inclusion in the operative paragraphs or with any assertion of priority. This contrasts with language in other resolutions relating to security.[55] A preamble may be a useful interpretative tool but, as Sir Michael

[48] Brown, 'The Securitisation of Human Rights', in J. Steans and D. Tepe-Belfrage (eds), *Handbook on Gender in World Politics* (2016) 255.

[49] The High-level Review was convened in accordance with SC Res. 2122 (2013) para. 15.

[50] n. 4.

[51] Security Council Open Debate on Women, Peace and Security, 13 October 2015, 'Gender Analysis', http://www.peacewomen.org/security-council/security-council-open-debate-women-peace-and-security-october-2015-0.

[52] SC Res. 1889 (2009); SC Res. 2122 (2013).

[53] SC Res. 1820 (2008); SC Res. 1888 (2009); SC Res. 2242 (2015).

[54] SC Res. 1960 (2010); SC Res. 2106 (2013).

[55] E.g. in SC Res, 1373 (2001) states are called upon to 'Become parties as soon as possible to the relevant international conventions and protocols relating to terrorism, including the International Convention for the Suppression of the Financing of Terrorism of 9 December 1999'; and in SC Res. 2331 (2016) to 'consider as a matter of priority ratifying or acceding to and to fully implement the United Nations Convention Against Transnational Organized Crime and its Protocol to Prevent, Suppress and Punish Trafficking in Persons, Especially Women and Children'.

Wood has warned, it should be treated with caution as preambles 'tend to be used as a dumping ground for proposals that are not acceptable in the operative paragraphs'.[56] It is also worth noting that the preambles in WPS resolutions have become steadily longer as more issues have been brought within the rubric of WPS but without further amplification in the operative paragraphs.

Second, the fourth WPS pillar relates to the relief and recovery of survivors—immediate emergency care and more long-term rehabilitation within the context of societal reconstruction. In Resolution 1325 such measures are described in terms of the 'special needs' of women[57] and in subsequent resolutions in the language of humanitarianism, of assistance to survivors of sexual violence, or of services that states are encouraged to provide.[58] They are not identified as rights. To take one example, Resolution 2106 (2013) recognizes the importance of providing timely assistance to survivors of sexual violence and urges provision of 'non-discriminatory and comprehensive health services, including sexual and reproductive health, psychosocial, legal, and livelihood support and other multi-sectoral services'. What is called for—non-discriminatory healthcare and other services such as access to sanitation, shelter, food, and livelihoods—are economic and social rights applicable under a slew of international human rights treaties, including the Covenant on Economic, Social and Cultural Rights (ICESCR),[59] CEDAW, CRC, and regional treaties such as the African Charter on Peoples' and Human Rights,[60] and its Protocol on the Rights of Women in Africa.[61] These treaties continue to be applicable in conflict and make no provision for derogation. The entitlements under these treaties are for all persons not just survivors of sexual violence.[62] Nor are they simply to confer humanitarian relief but are essential prerequisites for equal access to justice for crimes of sexual violence, a core component of WPS since Resolution 1820.[63] Failure to ensure economic, social and cultural rights undermines stability and human security post-conflict, which in turn lessens the ability or willingness of victims and witnesses to participate in the formal processes of post-conflict justice.[64] It also heightens women's and girls' vulnerability

[56] Wood, 'The Interpretation of Security Council Resolutions', 2 *Max Planck Yearbook of United Nations Law* (1998) 73, at 87.

[57] SC Res. 1325 (2000) para. 8: 'Calls on all actors involved, when negotiating and implementing peace agreements, to adopt a gender perspective, including, inter alia: (a) The special needs of women and girls during repatriation and resettlement and for rehabilitation, reintegration and post-conflict reconstruction'.

[58] SC Res. 1888 (2009) para.13 is the first WPS resolution to address fully relief and recovery. States are encouraged 'with the support of the international community, to increase access to health care, psychosocial support, legal assistance and socioeconomic reintegration services for victims of sexual violence'.

[59] 1966, 993 UNTS 3.

[60] 1981, 1521 UNTS 217.

[61] Maputo Protocol, adopted Meeting of Ministers, Addis Ababa, Ethiopia, 28 March 2003; Assembly, of the African Union, 2nd Summit, Maputo, Mozambique, 21 July 2003, https://www.ohchr.org/Documents/Issues/Women/WG/ProtocolontheRightsofWomen.pdf.

[62] SC Res. 1889 (2009) para. 10 does encourage states to address the needs and priorities of all women and girls in post-conflict societies including 'better socio-economic conditions, through education, income generating activities, access to basic services, in particular health services, including sexual and reproductive health and reproductive rights and mental health, gender-responsive law enforcement and access to justice'.

[63] SC Res. 1820 (2008) para. 4: 'to ensure that all victims of sexual violence, particularly women and girls, have equal protection under the law and equal access to justice'.

[64] Chinkin and Rees, 'Exposing the Gendered Myth of Post Conflict Transition: The Transformative Power of Economic and Social Rights', 48 *New York University J. Int'l Law and Policy* (2016) 1211.

to further gender-based and sexual violence, including trafficking and sexual exploitation and abuse by peacekeepers and humanitarian workers. Economic and social rights are not explicitly recognized throughout the WPS resolutions adopted before 2015 and nor is it suggested that monitoring and reporting processes develop indicators relating to their implementation. It might not be irrelevant that the US is a party to neither CEDAW, the CRC, nor the ICESCR but is of course a permanent member of the Security Council.

Third, is the call in Resolution 2242 (2015) for the greater integration of the Security Council's policy frameworks for countering violent extremism and terrorism within WPS and for the Counter-Terrorism Committee and its Executive Directorate to integrate gender as a cross-cutting issue throughout their activities.[65] The Council highlights the differential impact of 'violent armed groups and actors'[66] on the rights of women and girls 'in the context of their health, education, and participation in public life'.[67] It also expresses its deep concern that gender-based and sexual violence form part of the ideology of some such groups and are targeted at women and girls to boost the group's recruitment and finances.[68] Sexual violence is thus a tactic of terrorism as well as of war and is manifested inter alia through rape, forced and child marriage, enslavement, and new forms of sexual slavery. Other forms of gender-based violence include restrictions on and targeting of girls' educational establishments, abduction of girls from schools, harassment and violence against women and girls in public spaces and refusing them access to public spaces thereby denying healthcare, education, and livelihoods.[69] Expression of the realities of terrorism and violent extremism for women is combined with the centrality of women's participation throughout WPS in the Council's urging of states and the UN system to 'ensure the participation and leadership of women and women's organizations in developing strategies to counter terrorism and violent extremism'.[70]

An account of women's experiences of conflict and violence rightly includes the actions of terrorist groups and those committed to violent extremism that were highlighted at the time of the adoption of Resolution 2242 by the actions of ISIS in its military operations across Northern Iraq and Syria.[71] But just as sexual violence as

[65] Countering violent extremism seeks to prevent and counter radicalization. It is 'a security agenda that recognises the danger posed by violent extremism to: international peace and security; fostering sustainable development; protecting human rights; promoting the rule of law; and taking humanitarian action'. Gender Action for Peace and Security [GAPS], *Prioritise Peace: Challenging Approaches to Preventing and Countering Violent Extremism from a Women, Peace and Security Perspective* (2018) http://gaps-uk.org/wp-content/uploads/2018/06/GAPS-report_Prioritise-Peace-Challenging-Approaches-to-P-CVE-from-a-WPS-perspective.pdf.

[66] This expression is preferred to 'violent extremism' (ibid.).

[67] Preamble SC Res. 2242 (2015); see also SC Res. 2331 (2016) in the context of trafficking in armed conflict.

[68] Preamble SC Res. 2242 (2015); preamble SC Res. 2331 (2016).

[69] Report of the Secretary-General, *Conflict-Related Sexual Violence* (2016), S/2016, 361, paras 19–22; see also Independent, International Commission of Inquiry on the Syrian Arab Republic, *They Came to Destroy: ISIS Crimes against the Yazidis* (2016), A/HRC/32/CRP.2.

[70] SC Res. 2242 (2015) para. 13.

[71] See also SC Res. 2331 (2016) which reiterates this aspect of SC Res. 2242 and makes the connections between human trafficking, sexual violence, and terrorism. The Special Rapporteur on trafficking in persons, especially women and children, has urged integration of trafficking in armed conflict with WPS through both its recognition as gender-based violence and the desirability of a shared human rights approach; Report to the General Assembly, A/73/171, 17 July 2018.

a tactic of war is limiting in its scope, so too is its description as a tactic of terrorist groups. It discounts state terror, the complex histories of political violence that are often rooted in colonial and neocolonial encounters, and human rights abuses committed in the course of counter-terrorism operations. These violations are amplified through war rhetoric and increased militarization in countering terrorism, both of which marginalize those who challenge or fall outside the boundaries of predetermined gender roles. Counter-terrorism and national security are used to curtail dissent or criticism of governments and those defending human rights, including women human rights defenders, are harassed as security threats.[72]

Linking WPS with countering terrorism and violent extremism risks co-opting women's organizations and leaders and compromising them within their own communities. The Human Rights Council Special Rapporteur on human rights and counter-terrorism has highlighted that this connection is rarely founded on rights to non-discrimination and equality 'but rather relies on the strategic rationale that it leads to a more comprehensive understanding of the causes of violent extremism and more localized and credible strategies for countering terrorism'.[73] This constitutes a worrying form of commodification of women. Nor, the Special Rapporteur adds, has there been any 'systematic monitoring and evaluation assessing the merits, impacts or human rights compliance of such programming'. It furthers securitization of the WPS agenda, may provoke further violence against women's rights defenders,[74] and add to women's insecurity. Promotion of women's human rights is an end in and of itself which requires decoupling from counter-terrorism and violent extremism policy and security concerns.

Fourth, in its later WPS resolutions the Security Council encourages women's empowerment,[75] which supports objectives such as conflict prevention,[76] maintenance of international peace and security, stabilization of societies emerging from armed conflict,[77] peace consolidation,[78] and countering terrorism and violent extremism.[79] This linkage essentializes women as peacemakers and again promotes other interests over women's access to and enjoyment of human rights.[80] Nor is empowerment explained beyond references to economic empowerment or how it is to be achieved. Empowerment is more than a matter of economics and is a strategy not a goal; the goal is, or should be, gender equality and women's empowerment is a strategy for its achievement. WPS Resolution 2242 (2015) welcomes the commitment to gender

[72] NGO 2020 Roadmap on WPS, file:///C:/Users/user/Downloads/2020%20Civil%20Society%20Roadmap.pdf.

[73] Report of the Special Rapporteur on the promotion and protection of human rights and fundamental freedoms while countering terrorism, *Human Rights Impact of Policies and Practices Aimed at Preventing and Countering Violent Extremism*, A/HRC/43/46, 21 February 2020, para. 40.

[74] Report of the Special Rapporteur on the situation of human rights defenders, *Situation of Women Human Rights Defenders*, A/HRC/40/60, 10 January 2019.

[75] Women's empowerment is introduced in preamble SC Res. 1888 (2009).

[76] E.g. preamble SC Res. 2242 (2019).

[77] E.g. SC Res. 2122 (2013).

[78] E.g. SC Res. 1888 (2009).

[79] E.g. SC Res. 2242 (2015).

[80] In contrast, Art. 3 CEDAW requires states to take all appropriate measures for the advancement of women 'for the purpose of guaranteeing them the exercise and enjoyment of human rights and fundamental freedoms on a basis of equality with men'.

equality and women's empowerment in the General Assembly's 2030 Agenda for Sustainable Development (the Sustainable Development Goals),[81] which are themselves grounded in human rights[82] but this connection is not reiterated in either Resolution 2467 or 2493, both adopted four years later in 2019.

Fifth, the WPS resolutions provide for a range of new positions in UN peacekeeping operations for the protection of women and girls from sexual violence. These include women protection advisers and teams of experts that work with national and local authorities on improving criminal investigation and prosecution, military justice, legislative reform, protection of victims and witnesses, reparations, and security sector oversight.[83] The team of experts is based in the Office of the Special Representative of the Secretary-General (SRSG) on Sexual Violence in Conflict that provides detailed information on the situation in conflict-affected areas in annual reports to the Security Council.[84] In 2015 the Council took account of other developments in its peacekeeping/peacebuilding architecture that directly referenced WPS: the Report of the Independent High-level Panel on Peace Operations[85] and the Report of the Advisory Group of Experts for the Review of the United Nations Peacebuilding Architecture.[86] The Council has drawn less upon, and engaged less with, human rights expert bodies such as the Human Rights Council special procedures or human rights treaty bodies. The Special Rapporteur on violence against women, for instance, considered the situation of women in armed conflict as long ago as 1998[87] and the CEDAW Committee has long raised the issue in its concluding observations to states parties' reports. Rather than seeking assistance in the experience of human rights bodies, the Council has urged technical training and assistance. In contrast the CEDAW Committee has recognized that WPS cannot be appropriately implemented except in accordance with the provisions of CEDAW and a substantive model of equality.[88]

3. A Contrasting Human Rights Approach to Women and Armed Conflict

The CEDAW Committee has not only recommended that state implementation of WPS reflect a model of substantive equality taking 'into account the impact of conflict and post-conflict contexts on all rights enshrined in the Convention' it has also offered its own analysis and recommendations with respect to women in

[81] GA Res. 70/1 (2015) 'Transforming Our World: The 2030 Agenda for Sustainable Development'; Goal No. 5: Achieve gender equality and empower all women and girls.

[82] Ibid., para. 10: 'The new agenda ... is grounded in the Universal Declaration of Human Rights, international human rights treaties'.

[83] UN Team of Experts on Rule of Law and Sexual Violence in Conflict, https://www.un.org/sexualviolenceinconflict/our-work/team-of-experts/.

[84] The SRSG on Sexual Violence in Conflict and the Team of Experts were both established pursuant to SC Res. 1888 (2009).

[85] A/70/95-S/2015/446, 17 June 2015.

[86] A/69/968-S/2015/490, 30 June 2015.

[87] Report of the Special Rapporteur on violence against women, its causes and consequences, Ms. Radhika Coomaraswamy, submitted in accordance with Commission Resolution 1997/44, Violence against Women in Times of Armed Conflict, E/CN.4/1998/54 26 January 1998.

[88] CEDAW Committee, General Recommendation No. 30 (n. 5), paras 25–28.

conflict prevention, conflict, and post-conflict situations.[89] The Committee's General Recommendation No. 30 reiterates that states' obligations under CEDAW remain applicable during conflict[90] and provides detailed guidance on the extent and implementation of those obligations, including the duty of due diligence with respect to the acts of non-state actors.[91] This chapter cannot capture in full the richness of the General Recommendation, but will briefly highlight how the Committee's rights-based consideration contrasts with the security-based orientation of the Security Council,[92] each approach grounded in its own respective mandate.

For the Committee women are rights-holders. Crucially, they are 'not passive bystanders or only victims or targets' in conflict but are active participants in various ways—as combatants, within organized civil society, as human rights defenders, in resistance, as heads of households, peacemakers, political leaders, caregivers. Rights under CEDAW appertain to all women (not solely to victims of sexual violence). The Committee also understands that women's diverse experiences of conflict and its aftermath, in conjunction with their multiple and intersecting identities,[93] require responses to be tailored to their specific situation. The Security Council does not similarly take account of the complexity of women's lives.

The Committee does not accept any precise distinction or linear progression between conflict and post-conflict, but rather acknowledges the uncertain trajectory between moments of relative calm and a resurgence of armed violence. For most women what is termed 'post-conflict' does not end the violence: 'the forms and sites of violence change … [but] all forms of gender-based violence, in particular sexual violence escalate in the post-conflict setting'.[94] Unsurprisingly therefore the Committee links the entrenched sex and gender-based discrimination that pre-exist conflict, impede women's enjoyment of their rights, and are causes of violence against women in everyday life to the violence that is exacerbated by conflict.[95] It also finds a correlation

[89] Ibid.

[90] The Committee had already asserted the continued applicability of CEDAW during conflict; CEDAW Committee General Recommendation No. 28 (n. 35) para. 11.

[91] States' obligation of due diligence to prevent, prosecute, punish, and make reparation for the acts of non-state actors is reaffirmed in inter alia UN General Assembly, Declaration on the Elimination of Violence Against Women, A/RES/48/104, 1994; Beijing DPFA (n. 16) para. 124 (b); Commission on the Status of Women, The Elimination and Prevention of all Forms of Violence against Women and Girls, E/CN.6/2013/L.5, 2013, Agreed Conclusions on the Elimination and Prevention of All Forms of Violence against Women and Girls, para. 16; CEDAW Committee, General Recommendation No. 35 (n. 39) para. 24.2. In treaty form in Art. 7(b) Inter-American Convention on the Prevention, Punishment, and Eradication of Violence against Women (Convention of Belém do Pará), 1994, https://www.oas.org/juridico/english/treaties/a-61.html; Art. 5.2 Council of Europe Convention on Preventing and Combating Violence against Women and Domestic Violence, 2011 (Istanbul Convention), CETS No. 210, 2011. The Security Council WPS resolutions make no mention of states' due diligence obligations.

[92] For detailed analysis of CEDAW General Recommendation No. 30 and WPS see A. Swaine and C. O'Rourke, *Guidebook on CEDAW General Recommendation No. 30 and the UN Security Council Resolutions on Women, Peace and Security* (2015).

[93] General Recommendation No. 30 (n. 5) para. 6 refers back to General Recommendation No. 28 (n. 35) where the Committee notes 'race, ethnicity, religion or belief, health, status, age, class, caste and sexual orientation and gender identity' as factors contributing to multiple and intersecting discriminations.

[94] CEDAW Committee, General Recommendation No. 30 (n. 5) para. 35.

[95] The Committee is in effect reiterating what was pre-figured at the Vienna World Conference on Human Rights and Cynthia Cockburn has termed the 'continuum of violence'; Cockburn, 'The Continuum of Violence: A Gender Perspective on War and Peace', in W. Giles and J. Hyndman (eds), *Sites of Violence: Gender and Conflict Zones* (2004) 24.

between an overt increase in gender-based violence and discrimination and the outbreak of conflict, thus seeing these as early warning signals relevant to prevention strategies. The Security Council is largely silent about prevention of conflict with respect to both an imminent outbreak and more long-term indicators such as structural inequalities and violence.[96] The Committee takes account of a range of areas—inter alia migration, access to land and livelihoods, justice, and nationality—where state discriminatory laws and policies heighten the risk of conflict-affected gender-based violations and makes recommendations. Most importantly the Committee does not evade the question of women's sexual and reproductive rights and asserts forcefully that healthcare must include family planning, maternal healthcare, safe abortion, and post-abortion care.[97]

The emphasis in the WPS resolutions on women in the security sector, on conflict related sexual violence as a weapon of war (and later a weapon of terror), and their near silence about conflict prevention, root causes of violence and of conflict-affected sexual violence, the political economy of violence and its role in perpetuating conflict and inhibiting women's participation, all contrast with the recognition of the pertinence of these (and other) factors by the CEDAW Committee in its General Recommendation No. 30.

The rights-based orientation is important. Human rights law provides the tools to challenge the structures of power and the intersecting and interlocking discriminations and gender stereotyping that perpetuate the gender-based violence that occurs in non-conflict situations and continues into conflict and beyond. It also sets out state responsibility for international wrongful acts attributable to the state, including violations of human rights committed by state agents or in which the state is complicit. In contrast the Security Council's WPS resolutions primarily look to individual criminal responsibility for combating perpetrator impunity. This is important but criminal justice at the national or international level has not achieved gender justice. Individual international criminal liability certainly should not be abandoned but focus on the individual perpetrator and even the command structure deflects attention from both the collective nature of such harms and from the underlying structural inequalities that foster displacement and violence.

The Security Council has developed a WPS agenda. Through its recent General Recommendations, the Committee too has developed a detailed agenda that has fleshed out CEDAW. It provides a comprehensive way forward with respect to states' obligations for combating gender-based violence,[98] including in conflict and other disaster-related contexts and climate change,[99] securing non-discriminatory access to justice,[100] and education for women and girls.[101] It has linked the Convention to

[96] The *Global Study* (n. 4) 195 identified two approaches: operational practical measures and structural long-term prevention.

[97] CEDAW Committee, General Recommendation No. 30 (n. 5) para. 52(c).

[98] CEDAW Committee, General Recommendation No. 35 (n. 39).

[99] See CEDAW Committee, General Recommendation No. 37 on the Gender-related Dimensions of Disaster Risk Reduction in the Context of Climate Change, CEDAW/C/GC/37, 2018.

[100] CEDAW Committee, General Recommendation No. 33 on Women's Access to Justice, CEDAW/C/GC/33, 2015.

[101] CEDAW Committee, General Recommendation No. 36 on the Right of Girls and Women to Education, CEDAW/C/GC/36, 2017.

another contemporary policy agenda—the Sustainable Development Goals—thus underlining to states parties that their legal obligations to address women's rights in all contexts from 'peacetime' to social unrest, to low-level political violence, to armed conflict are integral to achievement of a wider range of social goals.

4. Security Council Resolutions on WPS in 2019

There were no further WPS resolutions after 2015 until 2019 when the political climate had harshened with respect to women's rights with backlash against progress, opposition to women's and girls' equal rights,[102] rising violent misogyny,[103] and a growing number of brutal attacks on those challenging social gender norms including women in politics,[104] and women human rights defenders.[105] The negotiation of Resolution 2467 in April 2019 was controversial and it was the first WPS resolution not to be adopted unanimously.[106] It was followed by Resolution 2493 in October which was adopted unanimously, in 'a welcome return to consensus in the Council',[107] although only after difficult negotiations. Resolution 2493 is however bland and according to some states lacked ambition.[108] Its sponsor, South Africa, considered it pertinent to reiterate the WPS agenda and the importance of its implementation in the run-up to the twentieth anniversary of Resolution 1325 in October 2020. Significantly some representatives from civil society questioned the desirability of a WPS resolution that did not advance the agenda and even risked setting it back.[109]

Resolution 2467 has been strongly criticized by some women's NGOs as retreating from a robust statement of women's rights in conflict. Two issues were especially contentious during the negotiations: women's sexual and reproductive rights, especially abortion, and the word 'gender'. Sexual and reproductive rights had explicitly entered the WPS agenda in the operative paragraph 19 of Resolution 2106 (2013) that urges the provision of 'non-discriminatory and comprehensive health services, including sexual and reproductive health' to survivors of sexual violence. Resolution 2122, adopted later that same year, is more explicit. Its preamble notes 'the need for access to the full range of sexual and reproductive health services, including regarding pregnancies resulting from rape, without discrimination' but this strong wording is not repeated in its operative part. Resolution 2122 was adopted on the same day as

[102] HRC Res. A/HRC/41/L.6/Rev.1, 10 July 2019, Elimination of all Forms of Discrimination against Women and Girls, preamble.

[103] Ms. Mlambo-Ngcuka, Executive Director of the United Nations Entity for Gender Equality and the Empowerment of Women, S/PV.8649, 29 October 2019, at 6/33.

[104] Special Rapporteur on violence against women, violence against women in politics, A/73/301, 2018.

[105] Special Rapporteur on the situation of human rights defenders, situation of women human rights defenders, A/HRC/40/60, 2019.

[106] China and Russia abstained.

[107] Naledi Pandor in her capacity as Minister for International Relations and Cooperation of South Africa, S/PV.8649, 29 October 2019, 14/33.

[108] E.g. the United Kingdom representative, Ms. Pierce, expressed disappointment that 'the Council did not seize the opportunity to draft a resolution that was more ambitious in scope'. Ibid.

[109] Security Council Report, *In Hindsight: Negotiations on Resolution 2493 on Women, Peace and Security*, 27 November 2019, https://www.securitycouncilreport.org/monthly-forecast/2019-12/in-hindsight-negotiations-on-resolution-2493-on-women-peace-and-security.php.

the CEDAW Committee's General Recommendation No. 30 that directly upholds women's right to safe abortion services.[110] Neither Resolution 2467 nor 2493 refer directly to sexual and reproductive rights. In the Security Council debate following the adoption of Resolution 2493 the US delegate stated that it could not 'accept references to "sexual and reproductive health", nor any references to "safe termination of pregnancy" or language that would promote abortion or suggest a right to abortion'.[111] The context must be remembered: rape and sexual violence in armed conflict.

With respect to the latter—the word 'gender'—the Security Council has never offered any definition and uses it in practice to mean 'women'. The WPS resolutions make minimal references to men and boys[112] and none to persons who reject the gender binary. Nevertheless, some delegations feared its use would incorporate the rights of trans persons or uphold gay rights.[113] 'Gender' does recur throughout both Resolution 2467 and Resolution 2493 but the widespread and insidious 'gender ideology' that is being used to push back against women's rights in places as disparate as Eastern Europe and Latin America remains a major challenge.[114]

While there is certainly room for criticism, interpretation of the 2019 WPS resolutions read in conjunction with their predecessor resolutions (which have not been rescinded) and existing international law, allows for the reassertion of state legal obligations and corresponding individual rights.[115] Indeed it can be argued that by 'recalling' all previous WPS resolutions (Resolution 2467) and 'reaffirming' commitment to their implementation[116] (Resolution 2493) language from earlier resolutions on sexual and reproductive rights is retained. The preamble of Resolution 2467 recognizes 'the need for survivors of sexual violence to receive non-discriminatory access to services such as medical and psychosocial care ... and need to be free from torture and cruel, inhuman or degrading treatment, and that violations of the obligations on the treatment of victims can amount to serious violations of international law'. Human rights bodies have recognized that denial or criminalization of abortion can come within the prohibition of torture,[117] which is directly implicated here.

[110] CEDAW Committee, General Recommendation No. 35 (n. 39) para. 29(c)(i) recommends repeal of legislation that criminalizes abortion.

[111] US Mission to the UN, Explanation of Vote on the Adoption of UN Security Council Resolution on Women, Peace and Security at https://usun.usmission.gov/explanation-of-vote-on-the-adoption-of-the-un-security-council-resolution-on-women-peace-and-security/

[112] The incidence of sexual violence against men and boys is noted only in SC Res. 2106 (2013) and SC Res. 2467 (2019).

[113] CEDAW Committee, General Recommendation No. 35 (n. 39) para. 29(c)(i) recommends the repeal of legislation that criminalizes being lesbian, bisexual, or transgender.

[114] E.g. International Resource Center, 'Turkey, Poland Consider Leaving Istanbul Convention on Violence against Women', https://ijrcenter.org/2020/08/06/turkey-poland-consider-leaving-istanbul-convention-on-violence-against-women/. On 20 March 2021, a presidential decree announced Turkey's withdrawal from the Istanbul Convention.

[115] For a fuller discussion see C. Chinkin and M. Rees, *Commentary on Security Council Resolution 2467: Continued State Obligation and Civil Society Action on Sexual Violence in Conflict* (2019), http://www.lse.ac.uk/women-peace-security/assets/documents/2019/reports/WPS-Commentary-Report-online.pdf

[116] SC Res. 2493 (2019) para. 1 also urges states 'to fully implement the provisions of all previous Security Council Resolutions pertaining to the Women, Peace and Security agenda and to reinforce their efforts in this regard'.

[117] CEDAW Committee, General Recommendation No. 35 (n. 39) paras 16–18 and references cited.

Perhaps the concern about loss of sexual and reproductive rights in Resolution 2467 is overstated.

The Council has brought some human rights language into the WPS resolutions, albeit inconsistently, and by so doing it must be assuming the accompanying human rights obligations. There is for instance explicit human rights language in Resolutions 2467 and 2493. Resolution 2467 is for example the first WPS resolution since 1325 to make express mention of CEDAW in both the preamble and its operative paragraphs. It urges recognition by states of 'the equal rights of all individuals affected by sexual violence in armed conflict' consistent with their obligations under CEDAW and CRC. This inclusive rights language, consonant with the universalism of human rights, encompasses male victims of sexual violence, as is made explicit in a later paragraph, and those targeted for their sexuality or gender identity, which is not. Since the preambles of both resolutions note the CEDAW Committee's General Recommendation No. 30 the Security Council appears to be inviting the reading of WPS in conjunction with CEDAW, as the CEDAW Committee has long espoused.

Resolution 2493 calls for the promotion of 'all the rights of women, including civil, political and economic rights'. The last is especially surprising as women's economic rights have been previously unremarked. Remedies were first mentioned in WPS Resolution 1888 (2009), which urges states to ensure that victims 'receive redress for their suffering'. Four years later Resolution 2122 recalled the applicable provisions of international law on the right to reparations for violations of individual rights, language that is largely repeated in Resolution 2467. It implicitly recognizes that human rights violations are entailed and that under human rights law victims' rights to reparation are independent of any conviction of a perpetrator,[118] or cooperation with the authorities.[119] The CEDAW Committee recommends that reparations (restitution, compensation, rehabilitation) be 'adequate, effective, promptly attributed, holistic and proportional to the gravity of the harm suffered'.[120] Along with other human rights bodies[121] the Committee has developed the concept of transformative reparations for both the individual victim and the wider community in which violations occurred. Especially important is the inclusion of guarantees of non-repetition[122] that require the state to address the structural inequalities and fault lines that underlie the violations.

Resolution 2467 brings legal reform into WPS in new and innovative ways, which endorse the CEDAW Committee's General Recommendations No. 30 and No. 33 and could—if fully and effectively implemented—have dramatic consequences for how sexual violence is prosecuted at the national level. Operative paragraphs 14 and 15 address some of the obstacles that women face that prevent their access to justice. States are called upon to establish victim and witness protection laws; provide, where appropriate, legal aid for survivors; set up specialized police units and courts to address such

118 As is the case under Art. 75 Rome Statute of the International Criminal Court, 1998, 2187 UNTS 38544.

119 As is in practice often the case with trafficked persons.

120 CEDAW Committee, General Recommendation No. 33 (n. 100) para. 19(b).

121 See the overview in Report of the Special Rapporteur on violence against women, its causes and consequences, Rashida Manjoo, A/HRC/14/22, 23 April 2010, *Reparations to Women Who Have Been Subjected to Violence*.

122 Ibid. para. 19(f).

crimes; remove procedural impediments such as restrictive limitation periods for filing claims; and end discriminatory corroboration requirements that exclude or discredit victims' testimony within law enforcement processes. Such measures are crucial for equality before the law and transformative gender justice.

5. Institutional Rapprochement?

Through its adoption of thematic resolutions such as those on protection of civilians in armed conflict, children in armed conflict, youth and armed conflict, and WPS, the Security Council has somewhat blurred the UN institutional divide between security and human rights. The *Global Study on the implementation of Resolution 1325* asserted the need for intergovernmental bodies and human rights mechanisms to act in synergy to promote the human rights obligations of WPS.[123] This is in line with the CEDAW Committee's recommendation that the WPS resolutions be read in conjunction with CEDAW and there has been some interaction between the Council and the CEDAW Committee since 2015. In 2016 Spain and Uruguay convened an unprecedented Arria formula meeting to discuss how synergies between the Security Council and the CEDAW Committee could be advanced. While some states expressed reservations, there was support for the CEDAW Committee's reporting and monitoring mechanisms as appropriate for enhancing implementation of WPS and for mutual reinforcement of the agendas.[124] The *Global Study*'s recommendation was not confined to CEDAW but other human rights mechanisms have remained largely silent about WPS.[125] The treaty body reporting systems, along with other human rights monitoring processes such as the Universal Periodic Review, are admittedly weak but they do provide an entry point for civil society mobilization through shadow reporting. As Beth Simmons has argued, the strength of human rights may lie in their mobilizing force for constituencies for domestic reform[126] and bringing WPS into these procedures for constructive dialogue with states may be a step towards reclaiming the human rights character of WPS.

Another boost to greater coordination between human rights mechanisms and WPS is the Framework of Co-operation Agreement between the CEDAW Committee and the Office of the SRSG on Sexual Violence in Conflict.[127] The latter was established pursuant to WPS Resolution 1888 (2009) and is responsible for annual reports to the Security Council. The Agreement is a first between a Security Council–mandated body and a human rights mechanism and is aimed at creating sustainable peace by

[123] *Global Study* (n. 4) 350.

[124] PeaceWomen, 'Arria Formula Meeting on the Synergies between SC Resolutions on Women Peace and Security and the Convention to End All Forms of Discrimination (CEDAW): December 5, 2016', https://www.peacewomen.org/node/96803.

[125] The Special Rapporteur on trafficking in persons has recommended greater integration of WPS and measures to combat human trafficking through a human rights approach; Report of the Special Rapporteur on trafficking in persons, especially women and children, Maria Grazia Giammarinaro, Report to the General Assembly, A/73/171, 17 July 2018.

[126] B. Simmons, *Mobilizing for Human Rights: International Law in Domestic Politics* (2009).

[127] 16 March 2018, https://www.un.org/sexualviolenceinconflict/wp-content/uploads/frameworks-doc/auto-draft/Framework-of-Cooperation-CEDAW-20180316.pdf.

ensuring that the UN pillars of peace and security, human rights, and development are closely linked. The current SRSG, Pramila Patten, is a former member of the CEDAW Committee who was instrumental in the drafting of the Committee's General Recommendation No. 30. Personal commitment and expertise are often conducive to promoting institutional synergies.

Resolution 2242 in 2015 also opened the door for more civil society involvement through the Council's expressed intention to 'invite civil society, including women's organizations, to brief the Council in country-specific considerations and relevant thematic areas'.[128] Women including from conflict-affected territories have briefed the Council about their communities, often with significant risk to themselves, but it seems with little impact on the ensuing country-specific resolutions.[129] This represents a lost opportunity for bridging the gap between the New York–based Council and women on the ground where the objectives of WPS are most needed. The Council has been urged to reflect the information received from local sources in its resolutions and to follow up in its actions.[130]

These limited institutional innovations fall far short of the rapprochement looked for by the *Global Study*. But even these go too far for some members of the Security Council that view any tendency towards greater human rights integration in WPS resolutions as overstepping the Council's mandate. Russia, for instance in the Council debate following the adoption of Resolution 2493 felt it had to point out that the resolution 'is overloaded with issues relating to the protection and promotion of human rights, which the General Assembly and the Human Rights Council already deal with successfully and effectively'.[131] China too has warned that UN bodies should each play their own prescribed role. The Security Council's primary responsibility is for international peace and security; while it should coordinate with other UN bodies each should act within their own respective responsibilities and be cautious about setting up new mechanisms.[132] The implication behind these comments is that the Council should not move into new areas.

6. Conclusions

So where are we? Women human rights and peace activists mobilized in the 1990s to secure the adoption of Resolution 1325 but was it a strategic decision to engage the world's most powerful actors for advancement of women's rights in conflict? Or was it a misjudgement to rely on the Security Council thereby making human rights a hostage to geopolitical imperatives? Was it absurd to think that the Council—a state-centric

[128] Security Council, Rules of Procedure, in Repertoire of the Practice of the Security Council. New York: Department of Political Affairs—Security Council Affairs Division, Rule 39 allows the Council to invite persons to inform the Council or otherwise assist it in examining matters within its competence.

[129] S. Kenny Werner and E. Stavrevska, *Where Are the Words? The Disappearance of the Women, Peace and Security in the Language of the Country-Specific UN Security Council Resolutions* (2020), https://www.lse.ac.uk/women-peace-security/assets/documents/2020/Report-WILPF-LSE-Web.pdf.

[130] Ibid.

[131] Security Council, 8649th meeting, Tuesday, 29 October 2019, S/PV.8649, 31.

[132] Security Council, 7533rd meeting, Tuesday 13 October 2015, S/PV.7533, 21.

body that considers military intervention as the norm and with the world's leading arms dealers as members—could ever be committed to human rights, especially those of women in armed conflict? Can proponents of human rights take language found in one instrument—a Security Council resolution—and tie it back to a human rights context to reinforce state obligations, or does the institutional divide prevent this consistency? And any such attempt is made harder by fluctuating language in the WPS resolutions; it cannot be assumed that good wording in one resolution that civil society can mobilize around will be repeated in subsequent resolutions.

I don't have the answers. What we have is an international system based in militarized security that is prioritized over a human security approach that might be progressed through human rights, a system trapped in hierarchical power structures, and a civil society not quite ready to reframe the discussion for fear of this issue being 'downgraded' to human rights, and an overall failure to commit resources.

This system is, as we are seeing, vulnerable to rising populism, to the invidious effects of 'gender ideology' and an erosion of multilateralism. Adherence to international law is currently severely compromised and undermined by many of the most powerful states, constituting a significant threat to international peace and security. The WPS agenda, already poorly implemented, is inevitably further weakened as a result and to many this is exemplified by the resolutions adopted in 2019. But there are human rights entry points in both Resolution 2467 and Resolution 2493, which have been little noted in the concern about what was omitted. Mobilization now must be about grasping these entry points and engaging the human rights mechanisms in resisting the pushback against WPS. To quote the Special Rapporteur on violence against women: 'Independent women human rights mechanisms are part of the solution to "push back the pushbacks and keep pushing back"'.[133]

[133] Statement by the Special Rapporteur on violence against women, its causes and consequences, 20 March 2019, https://www.ohchr.org/SP/NewsEvents/Pages/DisplayNews.aspx?NewsID=24380&LangID=E.

4

International NGOs and the (Non) Mobilization of Human Rights in the Context of Climate Change

An Inconvenient Frame?

*Rebecca Lock and Lisa Vanhala**

1. Introduction

The philosopher Henry Shue argued in 2013 that climate change is 'the single greatest systematic threat to human society'.[1] In June 2019, Philip Alston, the UN Special Rapporteur on extreme poverty and human rights, noted that the world is at risk of 'climate apartheid' where the rich pay to escape the impacts of climate change while the most vulnerable bear the brunt of the consequences of the climate crisis.[2] In his report for the Human Rights Council, Alston concluded that 'human rights might not survive the coming upheaval' and called out the human rights community for its 'reluctance to engage robustly with climate change'.[3] In September 2019, the UN High Commissioner for Human Rights, Michelle Bachelet, told the Human Rights Council, 'the world has never seen a threat to human rights of this scope'. Considering the gravity of the threat of climate change to the realization of human rights, it is puzzling that many relevant international NGOs (INGOs)—who have a proven ability to play an agenda-setting role on the world stage—have not engaged closely or have been slow to address the interlinkages between climate change and human rights. Why do some INGOs mobilize human rights in the context of climate change whereas others do not?

* The authors would like to thank the EUI, the students of the Academy of European Law Human Rights Law summer school and Gráinne de Búrca for the opportunity to explore this topic. Comments from Elisa Calliari, Liz Fisher, Angelica Johansson, Katrina Wyman, and participants at the NYU book workshop (8 March 2020) and the Bonavero Institute of Human Rights Discussion Group at Oxford University (22 October 2019) greatly helped to improve this chapter. Thanks to Olivia Nouailhetas-Baneth and Friederike Hartz for their wonderful research assistance. Lisa would like to acknowledge financial support, including an ESRC Future Research Leaders Fellowship, grant number ES/K008153/1 and a European Research Council Starting Grant under the European Union's Horizon 2020 Research and Innovation Programme, Grant Agreement number CCLAD 755753. Any remaining errors and omissions are the authors' own.

[1] Shue, 'Climate Hope: Implementing the Exit Strategy', 13(2) *Chicago Journal of International Law* (2013) 381, at 383.

[2] Alston, *Climate Change and Poverty: Report of the Special Rapporteur on extreme poverty and human rights* (2019), https://digitallibrary.un.org/record/3810720?ln=en (last visited 24 October 2019).

[3] Ibid.

Rebecca Lock and Lisa Vanhala, *International NGOs and the (Non) Mobilization of Human Rights in the Context of Climate Change* In: *Legal Mobilization for Human Rights*. Edited by: Gráinne de Búrca, Oxford University Press. © Gráinne de Búrca, Rebecca Lock, and Lisa Vanhala, 2022. DOI: 10.1093/oso/9780192866578.003.0004

The warming of the earth as a result of over 150 years of greenhouse gas emissions linked to human activity has increased the likelihood and intensity of extreme weather events and slow onset impacts, such as sea-level rise. It is predicted to lead to widespread health impacts and irreversible changes to our ecosystems.[4] Without drastic action in the next decades, climate change will cause millions of people to be displaced and hundreds of thousands to lose their lives.[5] Yet despite over 50 years of scientific analysis, international negotiations and grassroots activism, the world shows no signs of cutting its emissions to safe levels within the required timeframe.[6]

As understanding of the scale and urgency of climate change grows, interest in the issue has grown exponentially in academic, political, business, media, and public discourse.[7] Within these diverse fields, climate change has been framed in many different ways: as an environmental, scientific, ethical, political, economic, or even religious issue.[8] Erving Goffman highlighted the importance of frames—which he defined as 'schemata of interpretation'[9]—in the way they focus attention on specific elements of an issue, while deflecting attention away from other aspects.[10] The processes associated with this framing activity influence how different actors engage with an issue and the types of solutions they identify.[11] Due to its cross-sectoral implications, addressing climate change often involves 'frame bridging', that is the 'linking of two or more ideologically congruent but structurally unconnected frames'.[12] Yet, at least in the Global North, the most common framing of climate change remains an environmental one, in which the issue is presented as affecting complicated weather patterns and ecosystems.[13] For many, this presents climate change as an 'un-situated risk' which lacks urgency and direct relevance to everyday life.[14]

However, since the turn of the century, the 'climate justice' frame has become increasingly commonplace in political, academic, and activist discourses.[15] This

[4] Intergovernmental Panel on Climate Change (IPCC), *Climate Change 2014: Impacts, Adaption and Vulnerability: Part A: Global and Sectoral Aspects* (2014), https://www.ipcc.ch/site/assets/uploads/2018/02/WGIIAR5-PartA_FINAL.pdf (last visited 12 October 2018).

[5] Ibid. 364; World Health Organization (WHO), *Climate Change and Health: Fact Sheet* (2017), http://www.who.int/mediacentre/factsheets/fs266/en/ (last visited 14 October 2017).

[6] See Schleussner *et al.*, 'Science and Policy Characteristics of the Paris Agreement Temperature Goal', 6 *Nature Climate Change* (2016) 827; Spash, 'This Changes Nothing: The Paris Agreement to Ignore Reality', 13(6) *Globalizations* (2016) 928; Sneddon, Howarth, and Norgaard, 'Sustainable Development in a Post-Brundtland World', 57 *Ecological Economics* (2006) 253.

[7] See Dalby, 'Climate Geopolitics: Securing the Global Economy', 52(4) *International Politics* (2015) 426; Janković and Bowman, 'After the Green Gold Rush: The Construction of Climate Change as a Market Transition', 43(2) *Economy and Society* (2014) 233.

[8] M. Hulme, *Why We Disagree about Climate Change* (2009).

[9] E. Goffman, *Frame Analysis: An Essay on the Organization of Experience* (1974) 21.

[10] Allan and Hadden, 'Exploring the Framing Power of NGOs in Global Climate Politics', 26(4) *Environmental Politics* (2017) 600, at 602.

[11] Vanhala and Hestbaek, 'Framing Climate Change Loss and Damage Negotiation in UNFCCC Negotiations', 16(4) *Global Environmental Politics* (2016) 111, at 113.

[12] Snow and Benford, 'Framing Processes and Social Movements: An Overview and Assessment', 26 *Annual Review of Sociology* (2000) 611, at 624.

[13] Pettit, 'Climate Justice: A New Social Movement for Atmospheric Rights', 35(3) *IDS Bulletin* 35 (2004) 103, at 102; Quinn-Thibodeau and Wu, 'NGOs and the Climate Justice Movement in the Age of Trumpism', 59 *Development* (2016) 251, at 251.

[14] Hulme (n. 8) 196.

[15] See Bullard, Johnson, and Torres, 'Addressing Global Poverty, Pollution, and Human Rights', in R. Bullard (ed.), *The Quest for Environmental Justice: Human Rights and the Politics of Pollution* (2005) 279; Della Porta and Parks, 'Framing Processes in the Climate Movement: From Climate Change to Climate Justice', in M. Dietz and H. Garrelts (eds), *Routledge Handbook of the Climate Change Movements* (2014) 19; H. Shue, *Climate Justice: Vulnerability and Protection* (2014).

concept links climate change to the global justice movements of the 2000s, and highlights that those who contribute least to climate change are most severely impacted and are most likely to be left out of climate policymaking.[16] The related human rights framing of climate change (HRCC frame) has also gained traction in recent years.[17]

An HRCC frame as an issue generally features at least one (but usually more) of the four following characteristics. First, an HRCC frame focuses on how the impacts of climate change can violate a range of legally recognized human rights, such as the right to life, food, and health. Second, this frame also highlights the importance of taking human rights–based approaches within climate policymaking and implementation, and insists that taking action on climate change (whether mitigating emissions or adapting to climate change impacts) is not an excuse for human rights violations.[18] Third, an HRCC frame broadens the range of procedural options, actors, and venues that should be engaged with climate change. Scholars and activists have pointed to the fact that international human rights compliance mechanisms are in many ways stronger than those within the United Nations Framework Convention on Climate Change (UNFCCC) system and that human rights norms can be useful in guiding the international community in how to fairly apportion responsibility for human rights violations. At a more fundamental level, this approach can be seen to provide a moral and legal basis for stimulating action and cooperation.[19] Finally, proponents of this frame argue that adding a human dimension can render climate change as an issue more tangible and urgent to non-experts. This has the potential to mobilize new audiences and integrate actors who have traditionally been uninterested or excluded from climate policymaking.[20]

Given the fact that leading INGOs have a proven ability to play an agenda-setting role on the world stage and considering how an HRCC frame has the potential to stimulate urgent and equitable action on climate change, we sought to explore why some relevant organizations did not seem to be engaging closely with this issue. By relevant organizations we mean organizations with a clear mandate to work on either

[16] See Black, Milligan, and Heynen, 'Solidarity in Climate/Immigrant Justice Direct Action: Lessons from Movements in the US South', 40(2) *International Journal of Urban and Regional Research* (2016) 284; Pettit (n. 13).

[17] For further discussion, see Aizawa, 'Staying Human-centric at the Intersection of Climate Change and Human Rights', 88 *Journey of Energy & Natural Resources Law* (2014) 86; Limon, 'Human Rights Obligations and Accountability in the Face of Climate Change', 38 *Georgia Journal of International and Comparative Law* (2010) 543; Schapper and Lederer, 'Introduction: Human Rights and Climate Change: Mapping Institutional Inter-linkages', 27(4) *Cambridge Review of International Affairs* (2014) 666; and Humphreys (ed.), *Human Rights and Climate Change* (2010).

[18] See S. Atapattu, *Human Right Approaches to Climate Change: Challenges and Opportunities* (2015); Knox, 'Climate Ethics and Human Rights', in A. Grear and C. Gearty (eds), *Choosing a Future: The Social and Legal Aspects of Climate Change* (2014) 22; Doebbler and Wewerinke, 'Exploring the Legal basis of a Human Rights Approach to Climate Change', 10(1) *Chinese Journal of International Law* (2011) 141.

[19] See Allan and Hadden (n. 10); Limon, 'Human Rights and Climate Change: Constructing a Case for Political Action', 33 *Harvard Environmental Law Review* (2009) 439; Pickering, 'Moral Language in Climate Politics', in C. Heyward and D. Roser (eds), *Climate Justice in a Non-Ideal World* (2016) 255; Woods, 'What Does the Language of Human Rights Bring to Campaigns for Environmental Justice?', 5(4) *Environmental Politics* (2006) 572.

[20] See J. Hadden, *Networks in Contention: The Diverse Politics of Climate Change* (2015); Nicholson and Chong, 'Jumping on the Human Rights Bandwagon: How Rights-based Linkages Can Refocus Climate Politics', 11(3) *Global Environmental Politics* (2011) 121.

human rights or climate change. We do not take a normative position on whether these organizations *should* be engaging with an HRCC frame. Rather, this study empirically looks at the extent to which the organizations engage with this frame and what lies behind this decision. We do this through an abductive approach that moves between existing theory and data to begin to construct an explanation for the variation we find.

In seeking to further develop a sociological–institutionalist approach to the mobilization of human rights, we explore the relevance of different organization-level factors. We find that while some features of organizational identity—that is, sector, type, mandate, and brand—are often evoked in interviews as a key reason for the non-engagement with an HRCC, none of these factors account for the variation in engagement that we see. One of the most compelling findings of this research is that the way staff *perceive* an organization's identity (rather than objective features of that identity itself) and its fit with the HRCC frame is influential in shaping whether and how an organization mobilizes on the issue.

We first engage with the existing literature on climate change and human rights and bridge this with research on legal mobilization by NGOs. We then lay out our methodological approach which examines five case studies and draws on data from a content analysis of their websites and interviews, with 25 research participants with expertise on the topic from inside and outside the INGOs being examined. We then present and analyse the results, showing the extent to which the organizations engage with the HRCC frame throughout the 13-year period we study. Through the interview data and informed by existing scholarly literature, we abductively explore factors at the organizational level—sector type, mandate, brand, structure and tactics, and the way these elements interact with the issue-specific attributes of the HRCC frame—to account for the variation that we find. Finally, we outline the contribution this research makes to our understanding of legal mobilization and outline several suggestions for future research.

2. Existing Literature

Despite a now voluminous literature on the influence of INGOs in international politics on one hand and growing scholarly interest in a human rights approach to climate change on the other hand, there have been relatively few studies bridging these two streams of research. By reviewing the literature, we are able to uncover some of the gaps and highlight the contribution we seek to make with this chapter.

A. Deploying a Human Rights Frame in the UNFCCC Context

In the literature on global environmental politics, several studies have shown how transnational advocacy networks (TANs) and INGOs helped insert concerns about human rights and social justice into the international climate negotiations. This research has suggested that INGOs used the perceived failure of the 2009 Conference of the Parties (COP) in Copenhagen to steer away from a cautious, scientific framing of climate change towards justice and human rights framings which they hoped would encourage more urgent and equitable climate action.[21] Quantitative research has shown a growth in the diversity and number of NGOs attending the negotiations. Muñoz Cabré found there was a 350 per cent rise in the number of rights and justice groups attending the COPs from 2008 to 2009.[22] Andrea Schapper used content analysis, case studies, and interviews to trace how an HRCC-focused TAN—the Human Rights and Climate Change Working Group, which is facilitated by the Center for International Environmental Law (CIEL)—applied different actors' influence, resources, and expertise to 'foster the institutionalization of human rights in the international climate regime'.[23] Recent research has suggested that the consistent pressure and advocacy tactics of these networks were largely responsible for the insertion of explicit human rights language in the preamble to the 2015 Paris Agreement.[24]

These studies provide nuanced analyses which successfully demonstrate how diverse coalitions of actors have engaged with the HRCC frame. However, they do not systematically differentiate between civil society actors, mostly discussing the influence and activities of the TAN as a whole, with the occasional example of an influential actor.[25] Scholars have noted the radically different ways in which actors participate in TANs, with some strongly pushing the network's agenda while others 'free-ride'.[26] They also point out that there are often fundamental differences of ideas, frames, and solutions between the actors in the same TAN.[27] All of this suggests that there is a need for further research to understand how and the extent to which some of the key players engage with the HRCC frame.

Another limitation of this research is that it tends to focus only on organizations' engagement with international climate governance. By focusing on only the advocacy side of NGOs' activities, which can be a relatively small part of their work, there is a risk of missing the bigger picture in terms of engagement with the HRCC frame.[28] For

[21] See Della Porta and Parks (n. 15); Hadden, Explaining Variation in Transnational Climate Change Activism: The Role of Inter-movement Spillover', 14(2) *Global Environmental Politics* (2014) 7; Nicholson and Chong (n. 20); Vanhala and Hestbaek (n. 11).

[22] Muñoz Cabré, 'Issue-linkages to Climate Change Measured through NGO Participation in the UNFCCC', 11(3) *Global Environmental Politics* (2011) 10, at 16.

[23] Schapper. 'Local Rights Claims in International Negotiations: Transnational Human Rights Networks at the Climate Conferences', in S. Duyck, S. Jodoin, and A. Johl (eds), *Routledge Handbook of Human Rights and Climate Governance* (2018) 43, at 53.

[24] See Allan and Hadden (n. 10); Bäckstrand *et al.*, 'Non-State Actors in Global Climate Governance: From Copenhagen to Paris and Beyond', 26(4) *Environmental Politics* (2017) 561; Kuchler, 'The Human Rights Turn: ENGOs' Changing Tactics in the Quest for a More Transparent, Participatory and Accountable CDM', 26(4) *Environmental Politics* (2017) 648; Mayer, 'Human Rights in the Paris Agreement', 6(1–2) *Climate Law* (2016) 109; Schapper and Lederer (n. 17).

[25] Carpenter *et al.*, 'Explaining the Advocacy Agenda: Insights from the Human Security Network', 68(2) *International Organization* (2014) 449, at 452.

[26] See Bäckstrand *et al.* (n. 24); Hanegraaff, 'Transnational Advocacy over Time: Business and NGO Mobilization at UN Climate Summits', 15(1) *Global Environmental Politics* (2015) 83; M. Keck and K. Sikkink, *Activists Beyond Borders: Advocacy Networks in International Politics* (1998); Murdie, 'The Ties That Bind: A Network Analysis of Human Rights International Nongovernmental Organizations', 44(1) *British Journal of Political Science* (2013) 1.

[27] H. Bulkeley *et al.*, *Transnational Climate Change Governance* (2014) 126; Gough and Shackley 'The Respectable Politics of Climate Change: The Epistemic Communities and NGOs', 77(2) *International Affairs* 77(2) 329, at 334.

[28] Quinn-Thibodeau and Wu (n. 13) 253; Scott, 'Evaluating Development-Orientated NGOs', in C. E. Welch (ed.), *NGOs and Human Rights: Promise and Performance* (2001) 204, at 210.

example, NGOs also provide information to governments, educate the general public, and work with organizations on the ground.[29] Indeed, many argue one of the reasons why NGOs are so successful at norm dissemination is because they can discuss solutions and promote action outside contentious political environments.[30] It is therefore useful to look beyond the UNFCCC context to fully understand whether and how INGOs are working with the HRCC frame.

B. Differential Mobilization of Human Rights in the Context of Climate Change

Many of the studies referenced thus far have been useful for demonstrating the strategies employed and some of the impacts of HRCC-related advocacy, but they do not indicate why the NGOs added this issue to their agenda in the first place, an omission typical of the NGO literature.[31]

One study that does address this issue is Lorna Gold's research from 2017 exploring why international non-governmental development organizations (INGDOs) do not publicly seem to be engaging with the climate justice frame.[32] She found that organizations gave agent-related reasons for their silence on climate justice, such as 'our supporters aren't interested' or 'nobody wants to fund it'. One advantage of Gold's study is that she does not select her cases on the dependent variable, that is she looks at INGDOs in general, and then considers whether they engage with the issue of climate justice, rather than only focusing on those organizations already engaging with the norm. However, Gold only looks at organizations in one sector, development, but the climate justice frame is also relevant to other sectors. This is reflective of a broader tendency in the literature on INGOs to treat all INGOs, or types of INGOs, as a homogeneous group, without differentiating between sector or organizations.[33]

[29] See Ausderan, 'How Naming and Shaming Affects Human Rights Perceptions in the Shamed Country', 51(1) *Journal of Peace Research* (2014) 81; Linos, 'Diffusion through Democracy', 55(3) *American Journal of Political Science* (2011) 678; Lück, Wozniak, and Wessler, 'Networks of Coproduction: How Journalists and Environmental NGOs Create Common Interpretations of the UN Climate Change Conferences', 21(1) *International Journal of Press/Politics* (2016) 25; Tarlock, 'The Role of Non-Governmental Organizations in the Development of International Environmental Law', 61 *Chicago-Kent Law Review* (1992) 61.

[30] See Abbott, 'The Transnational Regime Complex for Climate Change', 30(4) *Environmental and Planning C: Government and Policy* (2012) 571, at 568; Magraw, 'International Law and Pollution', 2(4) *Environmental Values* (1993) 371; P. Newell, *Climate for Change: Non-state Actors and the Global Politics of the Greenhouse* (2000) 130; Tracy, 'The Roots of Influence: Nongovernmental Organizations and the Relationship between Human Rights and the Environment', 3 *International Law and Practise* (1994) 21, at 28.

[31] As pointed out by C. Bob, *The Marketing of Rebellion: Insurgents, the Media and International Activism* (2005) 19; Carpenter *et al.* (n. 25) 449; Stroup and Wong, 'Come Together: Different Pathways to International NGO Centralisation', 15 *International Studies Review* (2013) 163, at 163.

[32] Gold, 'Are International Non-Governmental Development Organizations Fuelling a "Conspiracy of Silence" around Climate Justice?', 59(3–4) *Development* (2017) 243.

[33] But see Brockington, Scholfield, and Ladle, 'Anthropology of Conservation NGOs: Learning from a Sectoral Approach to the Study of NGOs', in P. B. Larsen and D. Brockington (eds), *The Anthropology of Conservation NGOs: Rethinking the Boundaries* (2018) 47, at 50; Luxton and Wong, 'Agenda Setting in Greenpeace and Amnesty: The Limits of Centralisation in International NGOs', 31(4) *Global Society* (2017) 479.

A cross-sectoral analysis, which treats INGOs as 'real-life, differentiated actors' adds a new perspective and richness to this topic.[34]

By overlooking a key step in the process of mobilizing legal norms and failing to account for variation among NGOs, we miss a crucial part of the picture of how INGOs shape and disseminate global norms. By only examining the norms that NGOs do pick up and propagate, or by making assumptions about the homogeneity of NGO behaviour, we hamper our ability to develop more robust explanations of how and why some norms emerge and diffuse whereas others do not.

Drawing on existing literature on legal mobilization theory, which seeks to account for why some groups mobilize human rights norms whereas others do not, can therefore contribute to our understanding of NGO behaviour and the diffusion of norms. Research on legal mobilization at the international level is long-standing in some areas of international politics but completely absent from others. The application of legal mobilization theory to the study of global environmental politics is relatively embryonic. By drawing on theoretical approaches in research on legal mobilization, the role of INGOs, and international norm diffusion, we are able to begin to develop a theoretical framework to explore why some NGOs mobilize human rights in the context of climate change whereas others do not.

Accounts of the mobilization of legal norms that focus on opportunities, incentives, and constraints which exist at the level of the legal and political system offer an important starting point for explaining who mobilizes the law and why.[35] However, they are less relevant here when studying non-court-based mobilization of human rights across a number of organizations that are generally situated within the same opportunity structures. Resource-mobilization theory suggests that the amount, source, and type of resources available to INGOs is the most influential factor in determining the issues it will pick up and propagate.[36] Recent research has developed sociological–institutionalist approaches to legal mobilization across countries by paying attention to agent-level characteristics related to identity, beliefs, framing, relationships, and the role of legal professionals and expertise, but this theoretical approach has rarely been applied at the international level.[37] Finally, many scholars recognize that the characteristics of an issue are an important determinant of how likely an INGO is to engage with it; this is referred to as 'the issue attributes approach'.[38] For example, attributes such as how complex, relatable, or emotive an issue is have all been cited as key to

[34] Stroup and Wong, 'The Agency and Authority of International NGOs', 14(1) *Perspectives on Politics* (2016) 138, at 138.

[35] See, for example, E. A. Andersen, *Out of the Closets and into the Courts: Legal Opportunity Structure and Gay Rights Litigation* (2006); Vanhala, 'Legal Opportunity Structures and the Paradox of Legal Mobilization by the Environmental Movement in the UK', 46(3) *Law and Society Review* (2012) 523.

[36] See Galanter, 'Why the "Haves" Come out Ahead: Speculations on the Limits of Legal Change' 9(1) *Law and Society Review* (1974) 95; McCathy and Zald, 'Political Opportunity Structures and Political Protest', 82(6) *American Journal of Sociology* (1977) 1212, at 1213; L. Vanhala, *Making Rights a Reality? Disability Rights Activists and Legal Mobilization* (2010) 22.

[37] See Taylor, 'On the Social Construction of Legal Grievances: Evidence from Colombia and South Africa', *Comparative Political Studies*, (2020); Vanhala, 'Is Legal Mobilization for the Birds? Legal Opportunity Structures and Environmental Nongovernmental Organizations in the United Kingdom, France, Finland, and Italy' 51(3) *Comparative Political Studies* (2018) 380.

[38] See Carpenter *et al.* (n. 25) 452.

whether that issue is likely to be added to an organization's agenda.[39] Although most scholars agree that issue attributes are important to agenda-setting in INGOs, there is no consensus on the extent to which this factor is influential over other factors.[40]

In order to address the gaps we have identified in the existing literature, we pose the following questions: is there a difference in the extent to which relevant INGOs engage with an HRCC? If so, what are the key factors explaining this variation?

3. Research Design and Methods

We use a mixed-methods comparative research design for this study. We selected five case studies of relevant INGOs across different sectors, conducted a content analysis of their websites, and interviewed 25 experts from within and outside those organizations (see Appendix 1). The five case studies we selected were Amnesty International ('Amnesty'), Human Rights Watch (HRW), Oxfam, Greenpeace, and WWF. We focus on their international secretariats as these headquarters dictate much of the agenda-setting and strategic direction of the movement as a whole.[41] We only selected INGOs which were amongst the largest and most influential in their sector to minimize (but not eliminate) the relevance of factors such as significantly differential resources, media attention, and global influence.[42] We also wanted to take a cross-sectoral approach, and so selected two environment INGOs, two human rights INGOs and one development INGO.

A. Document Analysis

As most INGOs' theories of change involve informing, inspiring, and mobilizing the public, their websites, and public reports are a key mechanism for achieving this, with the vast majority of the organizations' work being represented online in some format.[43] Therefore, analysis of documents found on websites is particularly useful for answering the first research question as it allows us to systematically measure our case studies' public-facing engagement with the HRCC frame.

This analysis first systematically scanned the annual reports of Amnesty International ('*Amnesty International Report XXXX: The State of the World's Human Rights*'), Human Rights Watch ('*HRW Annual Report XXXX*'), WWF Int ('*Annual Review XXXX*'), Greenpeace Int ('*Annual Report XXXX*'), and Oxfam ('*Annual Report XXXX*') from 2012 to 2019. For each case study, the keywords '*human rights*'/'*right/s*'

[39] Keck and Sikkink (n. 26) 26–27.

[40] See Carpenter *et al.* (n. 25) 466; W. Wong, *Internal Affairs: How the Structure of NGOs Transforms Human Rights* (2012) 187.

[41] See, generally, Luxton and Wong (n. 33); Stroup and Wong (n. 31); Wong (n. 40).

[42] See, generally, Bob (n. 31); Murdie (n. 26); Thrall, Stecula, and Sweet, 'May We Have Your Attention Please? Human Rights NGOs and the Problem of Global Communication', 19(2) *The International Journal of Press/Politics* (2014) 135.

[43] S. Lang, *NGOs, Civil Society and the Public Sphere* (2012) 178; Merry, 'Interest Group Activism of the Web: The Case of Environmental Organisations', 8 *Journal of Informational Technology and Politics* (2011) 110, at 121.

(e.g. Indigenous rights, women's rights, right to water) and '*climate change*'/'*climate*' (e.g. 'a changing climate', 'climate-induced natural disasters', 'climate crisis') had to be mentioned in the reports in connection to be counted in the analysis. Here, we systematically differentiated between substantive and passive links. Substantive mentions display direct connections between climate change and human rights, whereas passive statements only loosely link them. It is important to note that the number of times a term appeared, e.g. mention of 'climate change', in an Oxfam report, does not necessarily correspond to the number of connections identified. In some cases, for instance, keywords appeared multiple times within one page, but the content of that page was only counted as one connection as it referred to only one topic/theme/case.

We conducted similar analyses on articles, blog posts, press releases and reports across the five organizations' websites from 2007 to 2019, offering a slightly longer time horizon. We separated out reports from other types of website engagement as they tend to require a greater investment of time and resources. This method of triangulating across data sources offers a more systematic picture of the extent to which different groups have linked climate change and human rights, and how that has changed over time.

B. Interviews

We conducted 25 interviews with experts working both within and outside the NGOs to help determine in an abductive manner the key factors explaining the difference in INGOs' engagement with the HRCC frame and to triangulate our document analysis. We chose this method in order to access information that would be difficult to extract from other sources and that would not necessarily be in the public domain. For example, we questioned the participants about the extent to which the internal priorities of the organizations reflected the content on their websites. This helped to address a common criticism of website data, which is that websites only present a 'consciously self-tailored image' and therefore may not accurately reflect the focus, efforts, or activities within an organization.[44]

We interviewed a wide range of experts from different departments and authority levels within the case studies, including board members, chief executives, directors of campaigns and legal directors as well as campaign, policy, communications, and advocacy officers and interns. The group of interviewees was comprised of current and former employees of the organizations, as well as external experts who could offer a broader perspective on the subject. We initially targeted potential participants through emails, LinkedIn, or Twitter messages and through our personal network, and then used snowball sampling to acquire further interviews. All the interviews lasted between twenty and ninety minutes and were conducted between April 2017 and January 2020. Of these interviews, 14 were conducted face to face and 11 by phone. Participants were offered anonymity. We used an abductive approach to analyse the

[44] Luxton and Wong (n. 33) 493.

data, moving between existing theory and key themes in the data, developing a coding framework, and refining and revisiting the data as required.

C. Potential Limitations

It is worth noting the limits of our research design and methods. First, we are cautious about making any strong comparative or generalizable empirical claims based on this research design as the 'comparability' or 'substitutability' of these organizations is—in many ways—constrained. We would not necessarily expect all of these organizations to have the same likelihood of adopting the frame and so in some ways a singular research question masks the assumptions we make about what we expect to find.

Also, this research design suffers from what positivist-leaning scholars would characterize as a 'many variables, small number of cases' problem. Nonetheless, the research design offers useful analytical leverage with the two sector-based paired comparisons informed by an interpretivist epistemology which can help begin to untangle some of the external versus internal factors shaping variation in interest and engagement with the HRCC norm. The interpretivist approach allows us to recognize that the outcome of interest is in many ways co-constituted with many of the factors we are interested in, such as staff engagement, organizational identity, and issue attributes. Furthermore, we believe this collection of organizations is particularly worthy of attention given their prominence and political power. These large INGOs have a proven ability to influence the formulation, diffusion and implementation of global norms and any insights into their propensity to mobilize an HRCC frame are valuable and advance existing knowledge. We note also that there are many other smaller NGOs that have done much to lead the charge on advancing a human rights–based approach to climate change, for example, the CIEL which spearheaded a petition taken by the Inuit to the Inter-American Commission on Human Rights in the mid-2000s, and the Climate Litigation Network grew out of climate change litigation and particularly the seminal *Urgenda* climate case in the Netherlands. We are not able to explore in a single book chapter how all of these dynamics across the NGO landscape play out, but would suggest that it is likely that this political ecology also plays some role in shaping the dynamics we are interested in.

Finally, one of the limitations of the content analysis concerns the fact that, despite all being leaders in their sector, some of the organizations are much larger and richer than others and they vary in their membership structures and mandates. For example, the budget and workforce of Oxfam is over five times that of HRW, and Oxfam and WWF's work includes on-the-ground service provision, whereas HRW, Amnesty, and Greenpeace focus more exclusively on campaigns, research, and advocacy.[45] As richer organizations have the resources to add more content to their website, this could inaccurately make them appear as though they are engaging more with the HRCC frame.[46]

[45] Human Rights Watch (HRW), 'Human Rights Watch, Inc. and Subsidies: Consolidated Financial Statements' (2017), https://www.hrw.org/sites/default/files/supporting_resources/financial_statements_2017.pdf (last visited 14 May 2018) 5; Oxfam International, 'Income and Expenditure' (2017), https://www.oxfam.org/en/annual-report-2016-2017/income-and-expenditure/income (last visited 12 May 2018).

[46] Thrall, Stecula, and Sweet (n. 42) 13.

While an imperfect measure, we compiled data on annual expenditure/expenses for each of the organizations to gain a sense of whether this might be shaping differences.

4. Discussion

The results clearly show that Oxfam and Greenpeace have historically been leaders in taking a human rights–based approach to climate change in their outward facing profiles (see Figures 4.1–4.3). Conversely, WWF (perhaps unsurprisingly given their emphasis on nature) has had very little engagement with the human rights frame during the whole period studied, and Amnesty also demonstrated a very low climate change engagement until 2017, after which it started substantial work on the issue. HRW also showed very little engagement with the topic from 2007 to 2014, after which this suddenly changed, with the organization demonstrating a further spike in engagement after 2017. Interestingly, Oxfam's visible engagement with an HRCC has fallen drastically since 2015, whereas Greenpeace's engagement with the subject has stayed consistently high.

This data is backed up by the information given in the interviews, as participants tended to reflect on the engagement with the HRCC frame of both their own organization and other organizations in a way which was consistent with one another and with the document analysis results. For example, all participants referencing Greenpeace highlighted its progressive work with the HRCC frame, whereas those working with and within Amnesty concurred it had a low engagement with the frame until 2017.

We now turn to address the second research question: why do some INGOs mobilize human rights to address climate change whereas others do not? We seek to

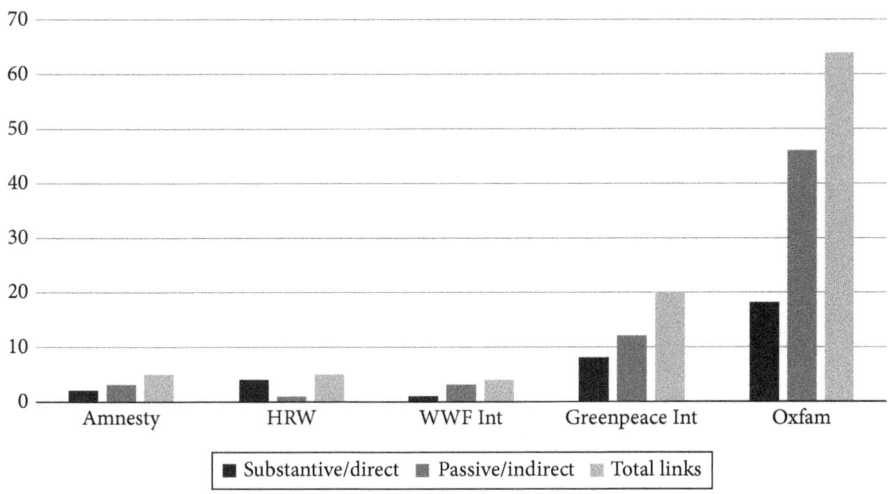

Figure 4.1 Linkages between mentions to human rights and climate change in annual reports 2012–2019

Source: Data gathered from organizational annual reports.

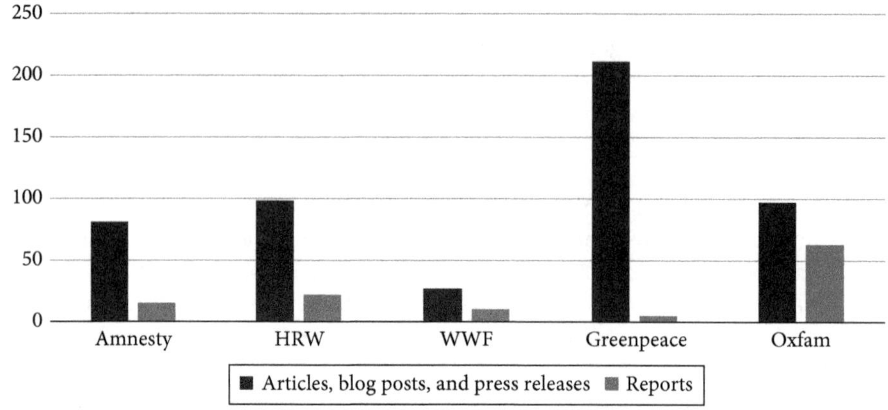

Figure 4.2 Number of articles and reports on human rights and climate change released between 2007 and 2019

Source: Data gathered from organizational articles, blog posts, press releases, and reports.

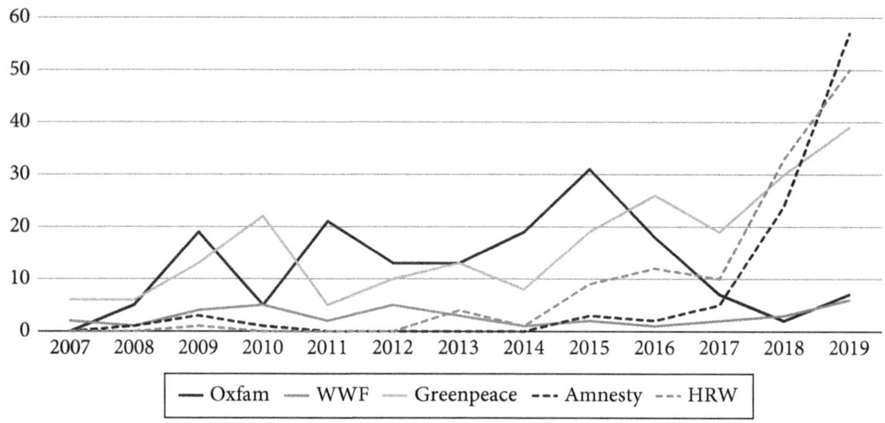

Figure 4.3 Number of articles and reports on human rights and climate change released between 2007 and 2019 over time

Source: Data gathered from organizational articles and reports.

develop the sociological–institutionalist approach by abductively exploring how agent-level characteristics and attributes of the issue influence adoption of the frame.

Existing literature on INGOs suggests that they are complex political entities in a resource-scarce sector, and so primarily make decisions based on a need to survive and thrive.[47] This literature would suggest that INGOs would adopt the HRCC frame

[47] Carpenter, 'Studying Issue (Non)-Adoption in Transnational Advocacy Networks', 61(3) *International Organization* (2007) 643–667; Wong (n. 40) 194.

depending on how well it fits with the NGOs' 'substantive, ethical, tactical and organizational features'.[48] However, our research found that it was INGOs' staff's perception or portrayal of these features (resources, mandate, tactics, etc.), rather than the features themselves, that seemed to shape their organizations' levels of engagement with the HRCC frame. We also found that willingness by key individuals within these organizations to actively push for the adoption of the HRCC frame mattered. We now explore the features mostly commonly cited as affecting INGO's engagement with certain norms—organizational identity, strategy, and structure—and then go on to consider whether the attributes of the issue also played a role.

A. Organizational Identity

Type, mandate, and brand are three concepts that are intrinsically linked and were frequently referenced by interviewees. We found that the way staff within an organization perceive and portray its identity is a key factor in explaining the difference in the INGOs' engagement with the HRCC frame.

First, an INGO's sector type, that is whether it is a human rights, development, or environmental organization, was regularly cited as a reason for not engaging (more) with the HRCC frame. There were many examples of what has been referred to in the literature as 'buck-passing', as in nearly every interview it was claimed that another type of NGO was better placed to engage with the HRCC frame.[49] For example, interviewees stated things such as 'this isn't Amnesty's business' (Interview 4) and 'human rights are dominated by so many other big players' (Interview 14). Even those organizations that demonstrated a high engagement with the issue seemed to think that they could not be leaders in the space as they needed to demonstrate 'humility' that other types of NGOs may know more about the subject (Interview 21), saw their role as more 'spotting opportunities where we can support' (Interview 25), or be 'humble enough not to waltz in like the 500 pound gorilla and pretend we know everything' (Interview 22). This silo mentality, where organizations do not want to work on anything perceived as outside their 'issue turf', inevitably mean that frames that bridge two issues, such as HRCC, are likely to 'fall between the cracks'.[50] Many studies have found this reasoning commonly employed when accounting for which issues an INGO picks up and which ones it does not engage with,[51] with Gold stating that that buck-passing is 'the most symptomatic and sector wide' rationale for inaction on climate justice.[52] However, our website analysis demonstrates that sector type did not shape patterns

[48] Bob (n. 31) 197.
[49] Carpenter (n. 47) 658.
[50] Carpenter *et al.* (n. 25) 466.
[51] Carpenter (n. 47); C. Carpenter, *'Lost' Causes: Agenda Vetting in Global Issue Networks and the Shaping of Human Security* (2014); Hall, 'Money or Mandate?: Why International Organizations Engage with the Climate Change Regime', 15(2) *Global Environmental Politics* (2015) 79; N. Hall, *Displacement, Development, and Climate Change: International Organizations Moving Beyond Their Mandates* (2016).
[52] Gold (n. 32) 246.

of engagement with the HRCC frame across these organizations, suggesting that, although frequently cited, this factor may not be as powerful in shaping difference in INGOs' engagement.

Second, organizational mandate, that is the declaration of their objectives and responsibilities, was also a commonly cited factor accounting for differences in engagement.[53] Nina Hall, in her study of issue linkage within international organizations (IOs), emphasizes how it is not the mandate itself, but the staff's ability to link a new issue to it, which determines whether the issue will be adopted. Clifford Bob names this 'substantive matching'.[54] These dynamics were borne out in our research, as well. For example, some interviewees from Oxfam and HRW remarked that it was easier for their organizations to engage with the HRCC frame because it was linked to campaigns they already ran, whereas staff from WWF and Amnesty mentioned that it was more difficult to find an 'entry concept' related to their current work (Interview 2). Perhaps for this reason, when discussing their lack of engagement with the frame, many interviewees stated that there were more 'central' issues to focus on first, citing that they needed to do 'less and better' (Interview 12), avoid the risk of 'spreading themselves too thin' (Interview 13), or 'focus on core issues' first (Interview 8). However, interestingly, when discussing dramatic jumps in levels of engagement with the HRCC frame with interviewees from Amnesty and HRW, no interviewees mentioned centrality to their organizational mandate or links to pre-existing campaigns in their reasoning.

Third, another factor frequently cited was the extent to which the HRCC frame was seen as diluting the organizations' brand. While 15 years ago the term 'brand' was considered too corporate for the non-profit sector, it is now part of the day-to-day lexicon of INGOs.[55] Indeed, brand consistency has been proven essential to the organization achieving political salience and generating funds.[56] It is therefore unsurprising that the organizations with the lowest HRCC engagement were most likely to comment that the HRCC frame did not fit with their brand. Interviewees from both Amnesty and WWF specifically mentioned the organizations' 'heritage' and 'roots' when describing their brand (Interviews 4 and 9), suggesting that the more an INGO feels tied to a traditional brand, the more difficult it becomes to expand its activities into other, non-traditional realms. However, again when considering Amnesty's sudden jump in engagement with the HRCC frame in 2017, this argument becomes less convincing.

B. Structure and Tactics

INGOs' structure and the tactics they typically deploy were also frequently cited as influencing the organizations' engagement with the HRCC frame. While many different aspects related to this area were mentioned, such as factors related to governance

[53] Hall (n. 51) 10.

[54] Bob (n. 31) 28–32.

[55] See Cottle and Nolan, 'Global Humanitarianism and the Changing Aid-Media Field: 'Everyone was Dying for Footage', 8 *Journalism Studies* (2007) 862; S. Hopgood, *Keepers of the Flame* (2006).

[56] See Cottle and Nolan (n. 55); Luxton and Wong (n. 33); and Wong (n. 40).

or the relationships with national offices, we focus on two characteristics most frequently cited by interviewees.

First, whether an organization has a formal membership structure was often cited as an important influencing factor by staff from Amnesty and WWF, the two organizations among our case studies which rely on their members to help effect their theory of change.[57] Participants from these organizations highlighted the importance of being able to clearly communicate any new issue in a way which would garner support and mobilize members, something which they claimed could be problematic in relation to the HRCC frame. For instance, interviewees from Amnesty mentioned that their supporters often see climate change as an environmental issue, with human impacts only occurring in the distant future. As one interviewee noted 'because the climate discussion started out as an environmental issue, and because when you think about climate you think immediately about carbon dioxide … and things like that … [it] seems pretty far away from human rights' (Interview 16). On the other hand, participants from WWF pointed out how an environmental framing of climate change, focusing on endangered species, elicits more support amongst their members than a human-centred frame. Finally, participants from both membership organizations raised how the HRCC frame made communicating solutions to climate change particularly problematic. Interviewees mentioned how, to maximize member engagement, you need to 'reduce the complexity of the issue down to one or two asks … that people who you want to be part of your campaign will immediately understand' (Interview 8). Therefore easy wins such as recycling or eating less meat could work well when looking at climate change within an environmental frame.[58] However, the HRCC frame highlights that a total and rapid overhaul of economic and social systems is the only way to prevent climate-related abuses from continuing, as incremental changes will not solve the problem quickly enough.[59] Participants from WWF and Amnesty stated that this makes the issue appear 'such an insurmountable problem that you can't actually take action on it' (Interview 14), causing member disengagement. One interviewee commented, 'stopping the death penalty, it's very clear what type of advocacy and what type of engagement you need to do in order to put pressure on governments that still support it, the climate change issue is far more complex' (Interview 22).

Although it could be argued that communication issues like these would be a problem for any INGO engaged in public-facing work, they are particularly exacerbated when the INGO relies on its members' support, meaning apparently difficult-to-communicate issues are often left off the agenda.[60] As Gold notes, this promotes 'a kind of circularity where [INGOs] feed their supporters with the messages they expect to hear and ignore the most challenging issues'.[61] However, the case of Greenpeace appears to contradict

[57] See Luxton and Wong (n. 33); and WWF UK, *Join WWF Now to Help Protect Our Planet*, https://support.wwf.org.uk/join-wwf-as-a-member (last visited 27 August 2018).

[58] Cleary, 'What are the Grounds Needed for Dialogue?', in P. B. Larsen and D. Brockington (eds), *The Anthropology of Conservation NGOs: Rethinking the Boundaries* (2018) 244; and Della Porta and Parks (n. 15).

[59] Jayaraman and Kanitkar, 'The Paris Agreement: Deepening the Climate Crisis', 3 *Economic & Political Weekly* (2016) 10; Pettit (n. 13).

[60] Luxton and Wong n. (34) 484; Winston, 'Assessing the Effectiveness of International Human Rights NGOs: Amnesty International', in C. E. Welch (ed.), *NGOs and Human Rights: Promise and Performance* (2001) 25, at 31.

[61] Gold (n. 32) 247.

some of the above claims, as this organization demonstrates the highest engagement with the HRCC frame, and yet also relies on engagement with its membership in order to effect change.[62] Furthermore, Amnesty shows a sudden engagement increase with the HRCC frame after 2017, which interviewees said was extremely popular with supporters.

Second, participants also noted that the range of an INGO's tactics is an important factor explaining their difference in engagement with the HRCC frame. For example, some interviewees mentioned how the HRCC frame does not fit well with Amnesty's 'naming and shaming' methodology, which relies on NGOs exposing human rights abuses to invoke a negative global reaction, which then pressures the perpetrator to change its behaviour.[63] Amnesty mostly effects this change through direct action from its members, which raises awareness of the issue through the media and via other civil society groups.[64] The methodology works best when there is a clear human rights victim, violator, and violation, as this helps to tell a clear story in a form these actors can easily understand.[65] This is a form of 'symbolic politics', where individual stories can draw attention to a wider issue, often inspiring broad-based support.[66] Yet, as 'causing climate change' is not itself a human rights abuse, the specific violation and causal chain is hard to identify.[67] Similarly, the impacts of climate change are so widespread, unpredictable, and varied, it is difficult find a victim in the form of a 'solitary moral hero'.[68] Finally, the 'villain' is also difficult to identify as, on one hand, attributing an HRCC violation to the actions of a specific actor is problematic in legal, scientific, and ethical terms.[69] On the other hand, nearly everyone contributes to climate change in some way, which means supporters could face the uncomfortable realization that they could be seen as the villain. This could cause them to disengage with the campaign, as people predominantly support charities 'to feel good' (interview 15). This suggests that Amnesty's naming and shaming methodology is a poor fit for the HRCC frame, though the marked increase in engagement in the last three years suggest other factors clearly matter more in accounting for its HRCC engagement.

Although HRW also uses a name and shame methodology, the organization relies less on the media and the general public to pressure actors into changing, and instead engages in more advocacy and lobbying of governments and IOs.[70] This allows HRW to escape many of these tricky communication issues, as actors with more expertise in the subject are able to deal with more nuanced campaign

[62] See also Luxton and Wong (n. 33).

[63] See Ausderan (n. 29); Dietrich and Murdie, 'Human Rights Shaming through INGOs and Foreign Aid Delivery', 12(1) *The Review of International Organizations* (2017) 95.

[64] See Bassano, 'The Boomerang Pattern: Verification and Modification', 39(1) *Peace & Change* (2014) 23; A. M. Clark, *Diplomacy of Conscious: Amnesty International and Changing Human Rights Norms* (2001).

[65] Roth, 'Defending Economic, Social and Cultural Rights: Practical Issues Faced by an International Human Rights Organisations' 26(1) *Human Rights Quarterly* (2004).

[66] J. Joachim, *Agenda Setting, the UN and NGOs: Gender Violence and Reproductive Rights* (2007) 22; Keck and Sikkink (n. 26) 22; Snow and Benford, 'Ideology, Frame Resonance and Participant Mobilization', 1(1) *International Social Movement Research* (1988) 197, at 208–209.

[67] Knox, 'Human Rights Principles and Climate Change', in C. P. Carlarne, K. R. Gray, and R. Tarasofsky (eds), *The Oxford Handbook of International Climate Change Law* (2011) 213.

[68] Hopgood (n. 55) 6.

[69] See Atapattu (n. 18); Doebbler and Wewerinke (n. 18); and Knox (n. 67).

[70] Brown, 'Human Rights Watch: An Overview', in C. E. Welch (ed.), *NGOs and Human Rights: Promise and Performance* (2001) 72, at 73; Roth (n. 65); Wong (n. 40) 152.

messages.[71] Similarly, participants from Oxfam mentioned how the organization primarily uses the HRCC frame in its programmatic and advocacy work, which does not require the immediate support and understanding of the wider public. However, again Greenpeace varies from this pattern as it engages in strategies that are similar to those used by Amnesty and yet engaged extensively with the HRCC frame.

WWF also engages in a broad range of strategies, such as coalition-building and programmatic work. However, participants stressed that the more (small 'c') conservative approach of WWF puts more restrictions on these tactics, with one interviewee commenting 'we never actually pick fights with certain people, which kind of explains why we're always middle of the road' (Interview 14). Finally, Oxfam also engages in coalition-building across sectors and extensive programmatic work in collaboration with governments around the world, and yet still shows a high engagement with the HRCC frame throughout most of the time period studied. This suggests that variation in tactics does not seem to shape organizations' engagement with the HRCC frame.

C. Staff Pushing for Change

Interview data suggest that an important factor in accounting for engagement with the HRCC frame is the extent to which staff members push for change within the organization. Although this factor was mentioned less frequently than some others, it appears to be most consistent with the data and would explain why some seemingly similar organizations have such different HRCC engagement levels.

For example, the INGOs' staff had differing approaches to organizational identity. Some appeared to see the organizations' identity as fixed, whether through the lens of type, mandate, or brand. Others noted that identity is an evolving concept which emerges through deliberation with other actors.[72] This echoes the literature on issue linkages and frame-bridging, which emphasizes that these opportunities are not static and 'natural' but require a concerted effort to bring about.[73] For example, interviewees mentioned that the sustained efforts of several key individuals within HRW who actively worked to convince the staff and management that the HRCC frame should be adopted resulted in the creation of the Environment and Human Rights Division in 2017. Yet, one HRW interviewee noted that this was a continuous process rather than a foregone conclusion:

> You really need to convince your colleagues that what you're doing is really important and adds to our work and having these internal discussions and external discussions about the value-added. I think that's something that's ongoing and will be ongoing for some time.
> (Interview 7)

[71] Gough and Shackley (n. 27) 331; Quinn-Thibodeau and Wu (n. 13) 255.

[72] Hopgood (n. 55) 214; B. Parekh, *A New Politics of Identity: Political Principles for an Interdependent World* (2008) 29.

[73] See Hall (n. 51); Jinnah, 'Climate Change Bandwagoning: The Impacts of Strategic Linkages on Regime Design, Maintenance and Death', 11(3) *Global Environmental Politics* (2011) 1; Snow *et al.*, 'Master Frames and Cycles of Protest', in A. D. Morris and C. M. Mueller (eds), *Frontiers in Social Movement Theory* (1986) 133; Snow and Benford (n. 66).

Other data showed that while it may not be possible in the short term to shape organizational identity, staff can begin to engage with the HRCC frame through the way the work is undertaken. For example, a former Oxfam employee mentioned that the organization attempted to campaign on the HRCC frame in 2007, but when they struggled to engage audiences, the organization implemented a rights-focused climate adaptation programme instead. Then, after deciding to work more on the systemic reasons for inequality, the organization began focusing on climate governance. In an interview with an Oxfam employee in 2020, it became clear that the reason their HRCC engagement seemed to drop so quickly from 2015 was not because the organization was reducing its work on climate change, but because it was focusing more on the language of inequality rather than rights in much of their external climate communications. The interviewee also suggested that the organization wanted to use more 'positive' language to inspire behaviour change by some carbon-emitting actors; rather than accusing them of human rights violations. The organization wanted to encourage those actors to make a difference in the climate space (Interview 25). However, human rights were still a key motivator behind all these internal decisions.

We found that the attitude of the staff to communication issues was also important. While some participants stated that the HRCC frame was 'too hard' (Interview 13) to communicate, others took more of the attitude that 'campaigners should work around that, that's the bloody job of campaigners!' (Interview 1). For example, the willingness of Greenpeace's staff to work on difficult issues was illustrated by one participant, who pointed out that they were one of the first organizations to campaign on climate change in any form, making them appear 'the lunatic fringe' (Interview 4). Yet, rather than seeing climate change as an 'un-campaignable' issue, Greenpeace worked on a successful communication strategy, at which point many other INGOs followed their lead. Similarly, an HRW interviewee mentioned how it took the organization a few years to work up an official 'human rights' position on climate change, and that once they had done this campaigning on the issue became much easier and was well received. In fact, a repeated refrain from participants who worked on the HRCC frame was a variation on 'once you explain it, people get it' (Interviews 1, 5, 7, 16), suggesting that the frame may not be as difficult to communicate as some thought.

Finally, there was a clear difference between the organizations who saw their lack of expertise on the HRCC frame as a fixed characteristic, and those who saw it as changeable through the recruitment, training, and promotion of staff. Whereas some interviewees took attitudes such as 'I can't think of a time when human rights hasn't been in the frame ... it's just that we're not human rights experts so we're less likely to have seized on that as an opportunity' (Interview 10), others took a different approach. For example, one HRW interviewee said it was clear that at first many of its staff felt uncomfortable with how the climate change issue fitted with the organization's mission, and therefore HRW invested a lot of time internally training their staff on the topic. Perhaps as a result, an interview with an HRW employee some years later made it clear that staff from all around the organization were now taking it upon themselves to include a climate change lens in their work, even if they did not work in the Environment and Human Rights Division.

Nina Hall found that hiring new staff with specific expertise was vital for pushing IOs' mandates to incorporate climate change.[74] In the INGOs we studied, this

[74] Hall (n. 51) 149.

phenomenon was most striking in the case of Amnesty International, who hired Kumi Naidoo, the former executive director of Greenpeace International, as its new Secretary General in 2017. Until that point, the organization demonstrated very low engagement with the HRCC frame, but then it very quickly rose to become a leader in this space by the end of 2019. Speaking about this topic in 2020, one senior Amnesty interviewee said:

> [Kumi] is an activist, and he was appointed by the board to rattle the cage in that sense. He was very outspoken about the fact that he felt Amnesty continued to be quite inward looking and played it very safe in the way we ran our campaigns and designed our activism, and I think his personal conviction in the climate crisis is now the top priority on the world's agenda.
>
> (Interview 22)

This sentiment was echoed by many other interviewees who had seen a clear change in Amnesty's engagement with the HRCC frame since Naidoo's arrival (though with his departure in late 2019 there are important questions about the extent to which climate change will continue to be high on Amnesty's list of priorities). All of this echoes research that suggests that individuals are able to form and reform organizations as a key component of the 'dialectical process of change'.[75]

D. Resources and Issue Attributes

Finally, we briefly consider two other factors that existing research suggests can help to explain variation in organizational mobilization behaviour.

The first of these is resources. Figure 4.4 shows the annual expenditure/expenses of each organization, suggesting that there is little correlation between financial resources and the adoption of an HRCC frame. While some interviewees stated that the likelihood of gaining funding for an HRCC project could have some impact on the organizations' decision to work on the frame, most participants did not seem to think this would be a major issue if the organization decided to prioritize the issue. Indeed, those organizations already meaningfully engaging with the HRCC frame stated that they had no problem raising funds for the projects, with some even stating it had bought in new revenue streams. This suggests that resource-mobilization theory is not as relevant in accounting for issue mobilization among these organizations or on this issue.

There was also limited evidence to suggest that the specific attributes of the HRCC frame alone shaped variation in engagement levels. Although the nature of the HRCC frame was frequently cited in interviews as important to INGOs' engagement, this only appears to be the case in relation to other organizational characteristics. Interestingly, despite INGOs claiming that the gravity of an issue is a major factor in how they choose issues to focus on, we found little evidence of this in the simple fact that in any moment in the studied time period, the organizations demonstrated very different engagement levels with the issue, despite the fact that the human rights

[75] Vanhala (n. 36) 29

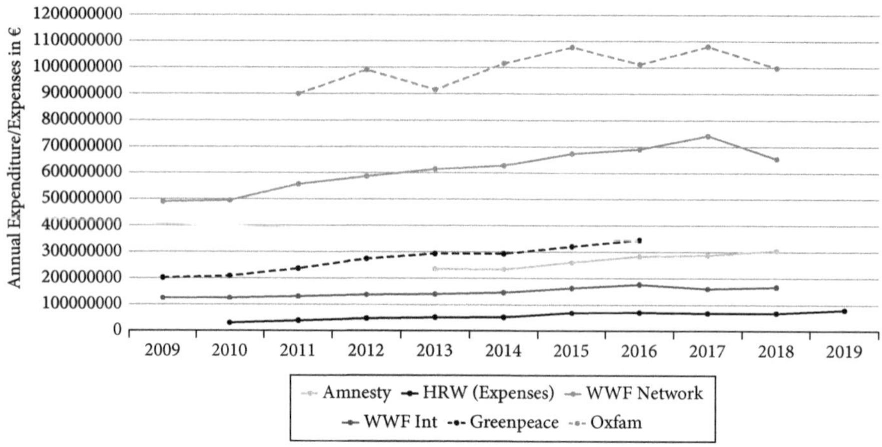

Figure 4.4 Annual expenditure/expenses

implications of climate change have been clearly visible for at least the last decade.[76] We therefore argue that the issue attributes approach on its own is unable to account for the differences in INGO engagement with the HRCC frame.

5. Conclusion

Overall, we found that there is a marked difference in the extent to which relevant INGOs engaged with the HRCC frame, and internal organizational factors were key to explaining why. In particular, we found that the extent to which staff perceive an organization's identity, strategy, structure, and expertise as fitting with the HRCC frame was especially influential. We do not take a normative position on this frame here, rather this research contributes to the development of a sociological–institutionalist approach to legal mobilization and norm diffusion which argues that organizational identity and ideas matter. Our research suggests that the most influential factor appears to be the extent of the staff's willingness to push for HRCC frame adoption internally, using tactics such as issue linkages, recruitment, and innovative strategies to change and adapt any factors that appear to prevent engagement.

Future research could further explore some of the arguments we have developed here using alternative methods, a broader range of organizations, or a focus on a different issue. One fruitful avenue of research would be to identify the necessary and sufficient conditions under which staff are more likely to be successful in pushing for an organization to mobilize human rights in a new substantive area. Intuitively, one might expect that organizations with closer engagement with lawyers—particularly with in-house legal staff—might be more likely to mobilize the law, but recent research has been inconclusive on this and has suggested that organizations have found a variety of ways

[76] Bob (n. 31) 198; Hopgood (n. 55) 210.

to find the legal support they might need.[77] What could be explored further is whether having senior leadership with a law or human rights background might play a role in shaping organizational culture to be more pre-disposed to taking a human rights approach to an issue. Finally, this chapter suggests that there is significant value in the work being undertaken to broaden our understanding of what legal mobilization outside of the courtroom looks like and how it shapes sociopolitical priorities.

Appendix 1

Interviewee Information

Table 4.1 List of interviewee numbers and date interviewed

Interviewee number	Date interviewed
Interview 1	8 June 2017
Interview 2	12 June 2017
Interview 3	4 August 2017
Interview 4	25 June 2017
Interview 5	28 June 2017
Interview 6	4 July 2017
Interview 7	19 July 2017
Interview 8	27 July 2017
Interview 9	10 August 2017
Interview 10	22 August 2017
Interview 11	24 August 2017
Interview 12	24 August 2017
Interview 13	4 September 2017
Interview 14	25 October 2017
Interview 15	9 December 2017
Interview 16	18 March 2018
Interview 17	19 April 2017
Interview 18	21 April 2017
Interview 19	24 April 2017
Interview 20	14 January 2020
Interview 21	16 January 2020
Interview 22	22 January 2020
Interview 23	23 January 2020
Interview 24	29 January 2020
Interview 25	24 January 2020

77 Vanhala (n. 37).

Table 4.2 Organizations at which the interviewees had worked

Organization (current or previous)*	Number of participants
Amnesty International	6
Human Rights Watch	2
Oxfam	7
Greenpeace	4
WWF	4
Other	5

*This amounts to more than 16 as several participants had worked at more than one of the case organizations.

5

Reframing Indigenous Rights

The Right to Consultation and the Rights of Nature and Future Generations in the Sarayaku Legal Mobilization

César Rodríguez-Garavito and Carlos Andrés Baquero-Díaz

1. Introduction

In June 2020, the leaders of the Sarayaku Indigenous people announced that they were going back to court. The judiciary had become a familiar venue for the Sarayaku. For 18 years, they pursued strategic litigation in Ecuador and the Inter-American Human Rights System to fend off the attempts of successive Ecuadorian governments to authorize oil exploitation in their territory, in the heart of the country's Amazon region. It was a remarkable journey that turned the Sarayaku into an icon of the rising global Indigenous peoples' movement in the early 2000s. It has also made them, since the mid-2010s, one of the key actors in the transnational movement for urgent action against global warming. Indeed, as government representatives met in Paris to hash out a global agreement at the 2015 climate summit, the Sarayaku leader Patricia Gualinga and other female representatives of the community pulled a publicity stunt by rowing down the Seine in a canoe that their community had built for the occasion from a giant Amazonian tree and shipped all the way to Paris, with the help of their international allies in the environmental and Indigenous movements.[1]

The use of legal tactics, institutions, and frames of mobilization has been central to the Sarayaku struggle. Notably, the Sarayaku legal mobilization included a nine-year lawsuit before the highest human rights bodies of the Americas—the Inter-American Commission and the Inter-American Court of Human Rights. The lawsuit ended with a 2012 landmark decision by the Inter-American Court (IACtHR) that ruled against the Ecuadorian state. In *Sarayaku v. Ecuador*, the IACtHR set a key precedent in international human rights law by recognizing that Indigenous peoples' right to free, prior, and informed consultation (FPIC) entails a governmental duty to meaningfully consult with and seek the consent of Indigenous communities before authorizing activities or issuing regulations that directly affect them.[2]

The IACtHR found that the Ecuadorian government had violated the Sarayaku's right to FPIC by granting a licence to an Argentinian corporation (Compañía General

[1] See 'The Living Forest: The Amazonian Tribespeople Who Sailed Down the Seine', *The Guardian*, 10 December 2015, https://www.youtube.com/watch?v=qzro0X4vCYU (last visited 7 December 2020).

[2] See IACtHR, *Case of the Kichwa Indigenous People of Sarayaku v. Ecuador*, Judgment (Merits and Reparations), 27 June 2012. All IACtHR decisions are available online at http://www.corteidh.or.cr/index.php/en/jurisprudencia.

César Rodríguez-Garavito and Carlos Andrés Baquero-Díaz, *Reframing Indigenous Rights* In: *Legal Mobilization for Human Rights*. Edited by: Gráinne de Búrca, Oxford University Press. © Gráinne de Búrca, César Rodríguez-Garavito, and Carlos Andrés Baquero-Díaz, 2022. DOI: 10.1093/oso/9780192866578.003.0005

de Combustibles (CGC)) to explore for oil inside their territory in 1996. Although the political, media, and legal campaign launched by the Sarayaku and their national and international allies managed to prevent CGC from drilling for oil in the Amazon, the company had illegally undertaken seismic exploration in Sarayaku territory, including through the use of explosives, without first consulting the Indigenous people. The IACtHR thus ordered the Ecuadorian government to pay reparations to the Sarayaku, remove the numerous undetonated explosives still buried in the jungle, consult with the Sarayaku before authorizing any further activity in their land, and issue nationwide regulations on FPIC in line with the Ecuadorian constitution, the International Labor Office's (ILO) Convention 169, and the Court's ruling. Although the Ecuadorian government at the time (led by President Rafael Correa) reluctantly paid the reparations and issued a half-hearted public apology in 2013, it failed to comply with the IACtHR's orders regarding the implementation and regulation of FPIC. Correa's successor, Lenín Moreno, had also failed to do so.

The Sarayaku, therefore, decided to return to court in 2020—this time to the Ecuadorian Constitutional Court—to demand that the government fulfil the IACtHR's orders. In a sign of the times, the press conference where the Sarayaku leaders and their lawyers announced the submission of the petition to the Constitutional Court took place over Zoom.[3] Beaming in from the Amazon rainforest and wearing face masks, the Indigenous leaders spoke not only of their legal claim but also of the fact that the ongoing Covid-19 pandemic and the floods exacerbated by the impact of global warming were severely impacting community members' lives and livelihoods.[4]

In this chapter, we analyse the Sarayaku campaign as a largely successful and iconic instance of transnational legal mobilization. Our study draws on a combination of qualitative sources, including ethnographic work in Sarayaku territory as well as interviews and participant observation with key actors in the case. Elsewhere, we present an in-depth case study of the campaign.[5] Here, rather than offering a detailed account of the political and legal twists and turns of the case inside and outside of Ecuador, our aim is to engage the broader scholarly debate about transnational legal mobilization in general and environmental and Indigenous legal mobilization in particular.

Specifically, we argue that a key factor underlying the evolution and remarkable impact of the campaign is the success of the Sarayaku coalition in contesting the narrow definition of FPIC and Indigenous rights advanced by governments, corporations, and international agencies such as the ILO. In contrast to the hegemonic understanding of FPIC as entailing purely procedural rights to participate in consultations, the Sarayaku have actively reframed the meaning of FPIC as entailing the right of Indigenous people to grant or deny their *consent* to new economic activities or regulations that affect them. More broadly, in terms of social movement and legal mobilization theory, the most impactful tactics of the Sarayaku people and other actors in the campaign can be

[3] See *In the Midst of a Critical Situation Due to Floods and Numerous COVID-19 Infections, Sarayaku Will Once Again Be in Court to Vindicate Its Territorial Rights* (2020), http://sarayaku.org/sarayaku-en-la-corte-constitucional-ecuatoriana/ (last visited 4 December 2020).

[4] Sarayaku Defenders of the Jungle, *Facebook Live Video* (2020), https://www.facebook.com/defensoresdelaselva/videos/983778225392613/ (last visited 4 December 2020).

[5] C. Rodríguez Garavito and C. A. Baquero Díaz, *Conflictos socioambientales en América Latina. El derecho, los pueblos indígenas y la lucha contra el extractivismo y la crisis climática* (2020).

construed as *framing* work. Mobilization frames are mental schemata that codify the experience of a social problem (like oil drilling in Indigenous territories) through legal categories (like the rights of Indigenous peoples and future generations) and offer an organized way of perceiving and responding to the problem.[6] The Sarayaku's framing tactics included: (i) reframing the legal dispute in terms of the rights of Indigenous peoples to self-determination and the rights of nature; (ii) communicating such frames in ways that resonate not only with courts but also with a broad global audience of environmentally conscious activists and supporters; and (iii) creating a bridge between the Indigenous rights frame and the emerging frame of global action against climate change.

As Lisa Vanhala has noted, legal mobilization scholars have devoted substantial attention to the role of legal rules in presenting activists with institutional opportunities for (or obstacles to) their claims. Hence the emphasis of the extant literature on legal variables such as ease of access to court, the permeability of domestic legal regimes to international human rights law, and the degree to which legal procedures enable the participation of affected individuals and communities.[7] This focus is also visible in the literature on legal mobilization around Indigenous peoples' right to FPIC.[8]

Far less attention has been paid to the equally important meaning-making dimension of legal mobilization, whereby activists engage with the law in order to shape their audiences' perceptions and understanding of the claims and the issues in question. We seek to contribute to the literature by focusing on framing processes and illustrating their workings with evidence from the Sarayaku case. We also discuss how the legal disputes and the outcomes of the numerous and protracted rounds of litigation revolved around the competing framings of FPIC. And we show that, far from passively importing the dominant frame of FPIC in international law, the Sarayaku and their legal advisers contested it and expanded and re-exported a counter-hegemonic frame that has influenced the evolution of global standards on Indigenous rights and climate action.

We further argue that the legal and political tactics of the Sarayaku campaign are characterized by a long-term perspective that is common in Indigenous peoples and environmental movements but has gone relatively unnoticed in legal mobilization studies. In analysing the evolution of the case over the course of almost two decades, we have deliberately chosen a longer window of observation than is currently utilized in case studies in the literature, which tend to focus on shorter episodes of mobilization. From this viewpoint, we seek to show that the choice of claims and tactics in the Sarayaku campaign is infused with a long-term vision that stands in contrast with the short-term temporality of the state bureaucracy and corporate targets involved in the

[6] D. Snow *et al.*, 'Frame Alignment Processes, Micromobilization, and Movement Participation' (1986) 464.

[7] L. Vanhala, 'Is Legal Mobilization for the Birds? Legal Opportunity Structures and Environmental Nongovernmental Organizations in the United Kingdom, France, Finland, and Italy', 51 *Comparative Political Studies (CPS)* (2018) 380.

[8] See, for instance, the important contributions by Falleti and Riofrancos, 'Endogenous Participation: Strengthening Prior Consultation in Extractive Economies', 70 *World Politics* (2018) 86; Falleti, 'Social Origins of Institutional Strength: Prior Consultation over Extraction of Hydrocarbons in Bolivia', in D. Brinks, S. Levitsy, and V. Murillo (eds), *The Politics of Institutional Weakness in Latin America* (2020) 253.

case. More generally, we argue that, just as legal advocacy studies have developed a nuanced understanding of space—for instance, by documenting how activists work at multiple scales by engaging in 'venue shopping' and alternating between domestic and international litigation—it also needs to incorporate a substantive and methodological awareness of the importance of *time* in legal mobilization. Sensitivity to time is especially relevant if we are to understand the mobilization logic and the outcomes of Indigenous and environmental movements, whose goal is to slow down, if not stop, the vertiginous pace of extractive economies, as well as to advance long-term goals such as the rights of future generations and the right to a liveable climate system.

2. Reframing Indigenous Rights: The Dispute over Free, Prior, and Informed Consultation and Consent

A. Between Consultation and Consent: Contrasting Legalities on Indigenous Participation

Since its incorporation into international law through ILO Convention 169 of 1989, FPIC has been a highly contested institution. As one of us has argued, the text and the practice of ILO Convention 169 are compromises between two contrasting views: (i) the procedural understanding of FPIC advanced by most governments and corporate actors during the negotiation and implementation of the Convention; and (ii) the substantive and empowered view of consultation and participation advanced by Indigenous peoples and their allies.[9] FPIC is a deeply controversial institution in which the dominance of procedural legality is constantly contested by Indigenous legal claims based on the principles of self-determination and the indivisibility of Indigenous rights, the rights of future generations, and the rights of nature. Each step taken to regulate FPIC or to put it into practice triggers this tension between neoliberal legality (which focuses on the *procedure* of consultation, as a manifestation of contractual freedom between supposedly equal parties) and the legality of Indigenous rights (which assesses the procedure in terms of its *outcomes*; that is, in terms of the degree to which it allows for Indigenous peoples to freely consent to or reject the project or decision under consideration as an expression of their right to self-determination and the duty to protect future generations and nature). The result of this tension is visible in article 6 of ILO 169, which states:

> In applying the provisions of this Convention, governments shall:
> (a) consult the peoples concerned, through appropriate procedures and in particular through their representative institutions, whenever consideration is being given to legislative or administrative measures which may affect them directly; ...

[9] C. Rodríguez-Garavito, 'Ethnicity.gov: Global Governance, Indigenous Peoples, and the Right to Prior Consultation in Social Minefields, 18 *Indiana Journal of Global Legal Studies* (2011) 263, from which this section is partly drawn.

2. The consultations carried out in application of this Convention shall be undertaken, in good faith and in a form appropriate to the circumstances, with the objective of achieving agreement or consent to the proposed measures.

As can be readily seen, this compromise solution conceives consent and agreement as a desired goal, as opposed to a requirement for the legality of a decision affecting Indigenous peoples. In a literal understanding of the text, the legally binding standard is the *procedure* of consultation, rather than the substantive outcome of it. This is the version of FPIC that has been incorporated into the constitutions or legislation of most of the 24 states that have ratified ILO 169 worldwide, including the 14 Latin American states that have done so.[10] More broadly, this hegemonic version of FPIC is a central piece of what Charles Hale calls 'neoliberal multiculturalism:' the legal regime that recognizes Indigenous cultural rights but denies, de facto or *de jure*, 'the assertion of control over resources necessary for those rights to be realized'.[11]

Contesting and expanding the meaning of FPIC has been a central goal of the transnational Indigenous rights movement. This was evident in the protracted negotiations that led to the adoption of a new international instrument on the matter, the UN Declaration on the Rights of Indigenous Peoples. Approved by the UN General Assembly in 2007, the Declaration embodies a hybrid approach. While upholding the hegemonic understanding of FPIC, the Declaration goes farther than Convention 169 in the direction of the Indigenous groups' proposal by requiring consent to relocate an Indigenous people from their territory.[12]

The dispute between the hegemonic and the counter-hegemonic understandings of FPIC has played itself out at the international and domestic levels, with different outcomes in different venues, cases, and countries. At the international level, for instance, the ILO guidelines have remained closer to the literal meaning of Convention 169,[13] while some human rights bodies, such as the UN Rapporteurship on the Rights of Indigenous Peoples[14] and the IACtHR,[15] have adopted interpretations of international law in general, and of Convention 169 in particular, that take the consultation requirement as the starting point but raise the bar by upholding the stricter requisite of obtaining consent when dealing, for instance, with large-scale development projects that may profoundly impact Indigenous peoples' lives and cultures. National governments and legal frameworks have also diverged in their interpretations of FPIC. For instance, while the Ecuadorian government and courts have traditionally defended a

[10] At the time of writing, 23 countries had ratified Convention 169. See International Labour Organization, *Ratifications of C169—Indigenous and Tribal Peoples Convention, 1989 (No. 169)*, https://www.ilo.org/dyn/normlex/en/f?p=1000:11300:0::NO:11300:P11300_INSTRUMENT_ID:312314 (last visited 4 December 2020).

[11] Hale, 'Neoliberal Multiculturalism: The Remaking of Cultural Rights and Racial Dominance in Central America', 28 *Political and Legal Anthropology Review* (2005) 10.

[12] Declaration on the Rights of Indigenous Peoples (n. 10) arts 19 and 32.

[13] International Labour Office, *Handbook for ILO Tripartite Constituents: Understanding the Indigenous and Tribal Peoples Convention, 1989 (No. 169)* (2013).

[14] Human Rights Council, *Rights of Indigenous People: Report of the Special Rapporteur on the Rights of Indigenous Peoples*, UN Doc. A/HRC/45/34, 18 June 2020.

[15] IACtHR, *Case of Saramaka People v. Suriname*, Judgment (Preliminary Objections, Merits, Reparations, and Costs), 28 November 2007.

procedural understanding of FPIC, the Bolivian government and the Colombian judiciary have embraced an interpretation that is closer to that of the IACtHR.[16]

For the purposes of this chapter, it is worth highlighting that ambiguities in international and national standards regarding FPIC are as much a trigger as a result of legal mobilization. Ultimately, the outcomes of legal disputes around FPIC stem from the opportunities and constraints created by the existing legal rules, on the one hand, and the subjective understandings and framing strategies of the actors that use them, on the other. Our interviews and ethnographic research show that the same rules (e.g. those of Convention 169) are invoked by broadly different actors, including Indigenous peoples, corporations, extractive industries' business associations, governments, courts, UN bodies, and international development agencies. The hegemonic or counter-hegemonic effects of those rules, therefore, are partly determined by the relative success of the competing framing strategies advanced by such actors in a specific legal dispute, as the Sarayaku case illustrates.

B. Between FPIC and the Rights of Nature: Framing Processes in the Face of Changing Legal Opportunities in the Sarayaku Case

Interestingly, the remedies that the Sarayaku leaders and lawyers sought in the aforementioned legal action before the Ecuadorian Constitutional Court were not focused exclusively on the implementation of the IACtHR's orders regarding FPIC. In their submission to the Constitutional Court in late 2019 and their public announcement after the Court admitted the case in mid-2020, the Sarayaku stressed that their ultimate goal was to get the Court to formally endorse their view of their Amazonian territory as a 'living rainforest' inseparable from human lives and cultures and, thus, as a subject of rights in and of itself.[17]

As noted, this type of reframing tactic has been crucial to the Sarayaku movement since its inception. Studies in framing theory have shown how social change partly hinges on whether activists manage to construct and reconstruct frames that give their movement an identity (*frame making*), so that they can have an echo with their audience (*frame resonance*) and so that they connect with narratives and agendas from other movements (*frame bridging*).[18] Evidence from three decades of social mobilization, including two decades of legal mobilization, shows that the Sarayaku and their allies consistently engaged in all three forms of framing work.

1. Beyond FPIC and Courts: Frame Making and Frame Resonance in the Sarayaku Campaign

The broader eco-centric frame predated the use of the specialized FPIC frame in the Sarayaku case by almost a decade. Indeed, the demands to protect the Amazon as a

[16] Falleti and Riofrancos (n. 8); C. Rodríguez-Garavito and C. Baquero-Díaz, *Reconocimiento con Redistribución: El Derecho y la Justicia Étnico-Racial en América Latina* (2015).

[17] Interview with Mario Melo, legal adviser to the Sarayaku people (27 August 2020).

[18] Benford and Snow, 'Framing Processes and Social Movements: An Overview and Assessment', 26 *Annual Review of Sociology (Annu. Rev. Sociol.)* (2000) 611.

'living forest' (*kawsak sacha* in the Quichua language) and respect the Indigenous worldview of a sustainable 'good life' (*sumak kawsay*) in balance with nature and the welfare of current and future generations were central to the mobilization of Amazonian peoples that marked the revitalization of the Ecuadorian Indigenous movement in 1992. In protest against the reluctance of the government of President Rodrigo Borja to formally grant collective land titles to Amazonian Indigenous peoples and exclude those territories from oil exploitation, the Sarayaku joined thousands of Indigenous protesters who walked the 350 kilometres that separate the Amazon from Quito. After one month of walking and another month of negotiations with the government, the Sarayaku and other communities were granted legal title over their territory.[19]

The march catapulted the National Confederation of Indigenous Nationalities (Conaie), which the Sarayaku had helped establish in 1986, to country-wide prominence. Through Conaie, the Sarayaku frame resonated with and had a direct influence on the national Indigenous movement and national politics and law at large. Marlon Santi, a former political representative of the Sarayaku, would even go on to become the leader of Conaie (2008) and later the head of Pachakutik (2016), the main Indigenous political party in Ecuador.

The Sarayaku mobilization helped shape the legal opportunity structures for and the framing of Indigenous rights in Ecuador at the turn of the century. The implementation of ILO Convention 169 was part and parcel of Indigenous claims throughout this period and led to Ecuador's ratification of the Convention in 1998 and the incorporation of FPIC rights into a new constitution in the same year. However, the Sarayaku people consistently advanced an expansive interpretation of FPIC, one that was not centred merely on consultation procedures but also on substantive claims about the incompatibility of extractive economies (like oil, mining, monocropping, and logging) with the rights of Indigenous peoples, the living forest, and future generations. For the Sarayaku, FPIC's rights holders are not only the members of their community, but also all other natural entities (from trees to rivers to animals) which are inextricably connected with human lives and cultures and whose survival is equally affected by extractive economies. As José Gualinga, then the political representative of the Sarayaku people, put it in our interview: 'in our community decisions are always made after consulting the living forest, analysing what it tells us and what all the people in the community have to say'.[20]

In fact, the Sarayaku legal mobilization can be best understood as a series of efforts to translate into law the principles of good living and the living rainforest. This leitmotif is evident in the key episodes of the case. For instance, in an award-winning documentary produced by the community's filmmaker shortly after the 2011 hearing of the case before the IACtHR, the Sarayaku introduced themselves to a global audience as the people 'whose life is the rainforest ... whose identity and beliefs are based on the living and spiritual beings who inhabit this forest'. This is also how José Gualinga introduced himself and his people at the beginning of the hearing before the

[19] D. Yashar, *Contesting Citizenship in Latin America: The Rise of Indigenous Movements and the Postliberal Challenge* (2005).
[20] Interview with José Gualinga in Puyo, Ecuador (2012).

full bench of judges in the IACtHR's chambers in San Jose, Costa Rica. 'We have come from the faraway territory of Sarayaku, from the river of maize; we are descendants of the jaguar', said Gualinga, alluding to the Amazonian archetypical animal spirit (the jaguar) and to the river that criss-crosses their territory and gives them their name (Sarayaku means 'river of maize' in Quichua).[21] Around the same time, the Sarayaku media team launched a website and a short documentary entitled *Kawsak Sacha* (living rainforest) that recounts the life and political and legal struggle of the Sarayaku in terms of the protection of all forms of life in the rainforest.[22]

The continuity of these substantive claims and mobilization frames is evident in the Sarayaku's renewed legal efforts in the 2020s. The ultimate goal of the petition before the Constitutional Court of Ecuador was to obtain formal recognition of the Sarayaku territory as a subject of rights.[23] As we will see, this request was grounded in the recognition of the rights of nature in the 2008 Ecuadorian constitution. For the Sarayaku, the petition was meant to translate into law their long-standing vindication of the rainforest 'as a living being, with consciousness, constituted by all the beings of the Jungle, from the most infinitesimal to the greatest and supreme', as spelled out in their 2018 Kawsak Sacha Declaration, which they invoked before the Court. In contrast to the human–nature divide that characterizes hegemonic understandings of human rights in general, and FPIC in particular, the Declaration claims that the living rainforest includes 'the beings of the animal, vegetable, mineral, spiritual and cosmic worlds, in intercommunication with human beings, giving them what is necessary to reanimate their psychological, physical and spiritual facets, thus restoring the energy, life and equilibrium of the original peoples'.[24]

It was this broader and longer-term view of rights that allowed the Sarayaku to contest the dominant FPIC frame, transform it, and re-export its modified version. Importantly, it was also that frame that allowed the Sarayaku to create bridges with the environmental and climate action movement. Frame bridging proved crucial to the success of their opposition to oil drilling, even in the face of variable and shrinking opportunities for mobilization in the Ecuadorian legal system, as we will show in the next section.

2. Forging Bridges, Expanding Opportunities: The Indigenous–Environmental Connection

The Sarayaku's expansive understanding of rights and FPIC opened the way for a key component of their legal and political mobilization: collaboration with a broad array of national and international allies well beyond the Indigenous rights movement. In addition to human rights organizations like the Center for Economic and Social

[21] See the documentary by the Indigenous Kichwa People of Sarayaku and Amnesty International, *Children of the Jaguar* (2013), https://www.youtube.com/watch?v=Ma1QSmtuiLQ (last visited 4 December 2020).

[22] See the documentary *Selva Viva, Kawsak Sacha* (2013), https://www.youtube.com/watch?v=LmJjQ6tYp_4&feature=youtu.be and information about Kawsak Sacha, *Kawsak Sacha, Sarayaku, Living Forest*, https://kawsaksacha.org/ (both last visited 4 December 2020).

[23] E. Laber-Warren, 'The Fight to Secure Rights for Rainforests', *Sapiens* (22 April 2021), https://www.sapiens.org/culture/eduardo-kohn-sarayaku/ (last visited 8 May 2021)

[24] See 'The Living Forest Declaration' in Kawsak Sacha (n. 22).

Rights (CESR, which represented the Sarayaku in their first lawsuit before domestic courts in 2002) and Amnesty International (which co-sponsored the documentary that introduced the Sarayaku cause to a global audience), numerous environmental organizations joined the call of the Sarayaku for the protection of the 'living rainforest', including Amazon Watch, EarthRights International, and Paroles de Nature.

Tellingly, the two organizations that provided expert legal support in the lawsuit before the IACtHR come from different backgrounds in human rights and environmental rights. Fundación Pachamama, at the time led by the Indigenous and environmental rights lawyer Mario Melo, succeeded CESR as the Ecuadorian legal representative of the Sarayaku. The international legal adviser in the case was the Center for Justice and International Law (CEJIL), the pioneer regional human rights organization specializing in the Inter-American system, led by Viviana Krsticevic. Melo has served as counsel to the Sarayaku for two decades, first out of CESR, later out of Fundación Pachamama, and more recently out of the Catholic University of Ecuador's School of Law. CEJIL and Krsticevic joined the case before the IACtHR and remained as international legal advisers in the enforcement of the Court's ruling. Indeed, both lawyers represent the Sarayaku in their new petition before the Ecuadorian Constitutional Court, which began in 2019 and concluded in 2021. For them (and for a generation of Latin American public interest lawyers), the Sarayaku litigation became one of the most prominent instances of the convergence of the Indigenous, environmental, and human rights frames.[25]

Key episodes in the Sarayaku story show how forging bridges across such movements had momentous consequences at the domestic and transnational levels. The clearest illustration within Ecuador are the debates that took place during the 2008 Constitutional Assembly, which resulted in the adoption of a new constitution that year. Interestingly, one of the most pointed disputes at the Assembly revolved around FPIC, to the point of creating fissures within the party of then President Rafael Correa.

Correa had been elected in 2006 on a leftist political platform and had been endorsed by Pachakutik, the Indigenous political party that had fared poorly in the first round of the presidential election. Correa's popularity gave his government the political capital to propose and win a referendum to convene a Constitutional Assembly, whose members were elected through popular vote and took office in late 2017. During the Assembly deliberations, it became clear that Correa's redistributive economic and institutional agenda banked on revenues from oil and mining, which had traditionally been the main exports of the country and whose prices were on the rise during the global commodities boom of the 2000s. Just like other governments throughout the region on both the left (e.g. Bolivia, Brazil, and Venezuela) and the right (e.g. Colombia and Chile), Correa clearly prioritized a conventional development agenda (through the promotion of extractive industries) over the protection of the environment and Indigenous rights. Indeed, Correa was one of the most vociferous critics of the environmentalist and Indigenous movement from a leftist perspective. As he put it in an interview for *New Left Review*:

[25] See n. 17

> It is madness to say no to natural resources, which is what part of the left is proposing—no to oil, no to mining, no to gas, no to hydroelectric power, no to roads. This is an infantile left, which can only legitimate the right. In the classic socialist tradition, I don't know where Marx, Engels, Lenin, Mao, Ho Chi Minh or Castro said no to mining or natural resources. This is an absurd novelty, but it's as if it has become a fundamental part of left discourse. It is all the more dangerous for coming from people who supposedly speak the same language. With so many restrictions, the left will not be able to offer any viable political projects.[26]

The rift between these two sectors of the leftist coalition that had supported Correa's rise to power and his referendum for a new constitution came to a head at the Constitutional Assembly. While the president and the majority of his party embodied the developmentalist left, Alberto Acosta (the Assembly's president and former Minister of Energy in Correa's government) and the Indigenous movement represented the environmentalist–Indigenous alliance. The latter's positions at the Assembly were influenced by the expansive interpretation of FPIC, human rights, and nature's rights advanced by Pachakutik and the main national Indigenous organization, Conaie, which at the time was led by Sarayaku leader Marlon Santi. Thus, the Constitutional Assembly was the crucible in which the connection between the Indigenous and environmental frames was consolidated.[27]

The text of the 2008 Constitution embodied a trade-off between the developmentalist and the environmentalist–Indigenous camps. On the one hand, the president's majority successfully quashed proposals for a constitutional provision on FPIC giving Indigenous peoples the right to grant or withhold *consent* and pushed through a narrow understanding of *consultation* (art. 57). On the other hand, Acosta, Sarayaku representatives, and other Indigenous leaders convinced the majority of the Assembly to recognize nature as a subject of rights (art. 11) and the pursuit of the Indigenous principle of 'good life' (*sumak kawsay*) as a constitutional goal (preamble) and as an individual right (art. 14) and duty (art. 83).

The compromise solution represented a tense and unstable equilibrium, one that has been at the heart of political and legal disputes in Ecuador since 2008. Ultimately, the Correa administration prevailed in prioritizing commodity-based economic growth and redistribution and managed to enforce its conception of FPIC and environmental and Indigenous rights. As the president gradually consolidated power, co-opted other state institutions, and persecuted members of the opposition, the narrow understanding of FPIC was enforced not only through the government's own policies but also through court rulings.

The key test case was the constitutional lawsuit brought by Conaie against the 2009 Mining Law that the Correa administration passed through Congress shortly after the enactment of the new constitution. Alleging that Indigenous peoples had not been consulted despite the profound impact of mining activities in their territories, Conaie

[26] Correa, 'Interview: Ecuador's Path', 77 *New Left Review (NLR)* (2012) 89, at 95.

[27] For a first-hand account of this convergence and its impact on the 2008 Constitution, see Acosta, 'Construcción Constituyente de la Naturaleza: Repasando una Historia con Mucho Futuro', in L. Estupiñán *et al.* (eds), *La Naturaleza como Sujeto de Derechos en el Constitucionalismo Democrático* (2019) 155.

petitioned the Constitutional Court to strike down the law. The Court, which had been created by the new constitution and staffed with a majority of Correa supporters, ruled in favour of the government, and embraced the hegemonic understanding of FPIC that would inform Ecuadorian institutions and policies until the end of Correa's decade in power (2017).[28]

Beyond the details of the case, what is important for the purposes of this chapter is that the Sarayaku mobilization unfolded in a context of unfavourable legal opportunity structures. As Tulia Falleti and Thea Riofrancos have documented, the increasing antagonism of the government and its eventual break with the Indigenous movement meant that the implementation of FPIC rules in Ecuador took place in a highly polarized environment in which the government ultimately had the upper hand.[29] This contrasted with other national settings such as Bolivia (where part of the Indigenous movement was incorporated into the Evo Morales administration) and Colombia (where courts were largely receptive to the counter-hegemonic understanding of FPIC advanced by the Indigenous movement).

The unpropitious institutional conditions for the Sarayaku and the Indigenous movement were not limited to unfavourable legal rules and court rulings. They also took the form of governmental persecution of leading organizations and individuals representing the Indigenous and environmental movements, including those involved in the Sarayaku case. In 2017, Fundación Pachamama was suddenly shut down by the government on unsubstantiated and vague grounds that, by opposing a new round of oil concessions, the organization had engaged in illegal political activities. Over the years after Conaie broke with government during the disputes around FPIC and Indigenous rights at the 2008 Constitutional Assembly, a number of Indigenous leaders were prosecuted on criminal charges of terrorism for convening protests against the government's developmental policies.[30]

In light of limited institutional opportunities, what explains the remarkable outcomes of the Sarayaku's legal mobilization? In the following section, we argue both that the answer lies in the combination of domestic and international strategies utilized in the case and that the framing processes discussed previously in this chapter were crucial to those strategies.

3. Reframing and Re-exporting FPIC: The Outcomes of the Sarayaku Case

The Sarayaku legal mobilization has succeeded in stopping multiple attempts to drill for oil in their territory over the last two decades. It fell short, however, of getting the Ecuadorian government to enforce FPIC in a way that is consistent with the IACtHR's ruling and their own expansive interpretation of Indigenous rights and the rights of nature. This was so even under the government of President Lenín Moreno, who

[28] Constitutional Court (Ecuador), *Sentencia 001-10-SIN-CC* (2010).

[29] Falleti and Riofrancos (n. 8).

[30] I. Caselli, 'Ecuador President Rafael Correa Loses Indigenous Allies', 19 April 2011, https://www.bbc.com/news/world-latin-america-12944231 (last visited 7 December 2020).

replaced Correa, put an end to the persecution of the Indigenous and environmental leaders, and restored judicial independence.

Nevertheless, when viewed from an international perspective and a longer perspective, the outcomes of the Sarayaku case go well beyond oil exploitation in the Amazon and the regulation of FPIC. Indeed, the case has not only helped shape international legal standards on FPIC but also has reframed the debate on FPIC in the direction of the counter-hegemonic understanding of consultation and consent that the Sarayaku and the Indigenous movement have proposed—that is, as part of an expansive understanding of human rights, the rights of nature, and the rights of future generations. This understanding, in turn, has had an impact on the global movement for climate action. In this section, we close our case study by examining how the framing strategies of the campaign influenced the rules and the understanding of FPIC at the international level.

A. Globalizing the Vernacular: The Influence of the Sarayaku Case on International Law

Shortly before the IACtHR was to deliver its ruling, then President Correa put the contrast between the government's and the Sarayaku's interpretation of FPIC in the starkest possible terms. 'Some believe that consultation is permission from the community', said Correa:

> No! Prior consultation is socializing, it is seeking to reach an agreement, an understanding. If all of this is achieved, all the better, but if it is not achieved, in accordance with international law and the Constitution of the Republic, the President can take the decisions for which he has authority . . . Prior consultation does not imply the imposition of the will of indigenous peoples on the State.[31]

In its landmark decision in the case, the IACtHR split the difference between the two visions of FPIC. As a result, relative to the prevailing understanding of FPIC in Ecuador and most other countries, it considerably moved the compromise solution in the direction of the Indigenous people's position. It upheld, as a general rule, the procedural understanding of FPIC while also establishing an important generic exception for situations in which the physical or cultural integrity of affected Indigenous communities may be compromised. In these especially serious cases, the Court stated that *consent*, not consultation, is the adequate standard. Since no consultation had taken place in the Sarayaku case, and no oil project undertaken, the Court ruled that:

> [t]he State must consult the Sarayaku People in a prior, adequate and effective manner, and in full compliance with the relevant international standards applicable, in the event that it seeks to carry out any activity or project for the extraction of

[31] P. Mena Erazo, *Censura a Ecuador por un contrato de extracción en tierra indígena*, 9 August 2012, https://elpais.com/internacional/2012/08/09/actualidad/1344546763_500362.html (last visited 7 December 2020).

natural resources on its territory, or any investment or development plan of any other type that could involve a potential impact on their territory.[32]

Although the IACtHR had laid the foundation for this interpretation of international and Inter-American law in previous cases,[33] the Sarayaku ruling has been by far the most visible and influential decision on Indigenous rights in the continent, and it's widely cited as a key precedent in international law. The case thus represents an instance of globalization of law from below: from the local to the global, from the South to the North. One of us has called this type of reverse legal export the 'globalization of the legal vernacular'[34] to contrast it with the well-studied processes running in the opposite direction, which Sally Merry aptly called 'vernacularization':[35] the global dissemination of norms created in global venues such as the UN or in Global North jurisdictions and then spread and imported at the domestic scale around the world.

Instead of simply importing and 'vernacularizing' the international FPIC frame into their local struggles, the Sarayaku have transformed and re-exported it to a range of hard law and soft law institutions, from the Inter-American system to the UN Special Rapporteurship on the rights of Indigenous peoples. The Sarayaku community and its lawsuit were instrumental in the emergence of the non-governmental International Rights of Nature Tribunal, hosted by the Global Alliance for the Rights of Nature. Partly for this reason, the Tribunal's first session took place in Quito in 2014, during the Global Rights of Nature Summit. The second session overlapped with COP20 in Lima in December 2014, and the third took place during COP21 in Paris in December 2015. In Paris, one of the cases heard by the Tribunal was that of the Sarayaku. Addressing the Tribunal, José Gualinga argued that if there is a continuity between human beings and nature, and non-human nature is also alive, then those other living beings should also be consulted. As noted, this is precisely what his people had been arguing for a quarter of a century, ever since FPIC became prominent in debates on Indigenous peoples' rights in Ecuador, and elsewhere.

B. Bridging Global Frames: From Indigenous Rights to the Rights of Nature and Climate Action

As noted, the Sarayaku mobilization built bridges between the Indigenous and the environmental rights agendas in Ecuador and became an icon of this convergence within Latin America at large. In a telling illustration of how the case forged further connections across movements and borders, a delegation of the Sarayaku community participated in the Standing Rock protests in solidarity with the Lakota people of the United States. In the winter of 2016–2017, the Lakota led the largest contemporary

[32] See *Case of the Kichwa Indigenous People of Sarayaku v. Ecuador* (n. 2) at Order para. 3.

[33] *Case of Saramaka People v. Suriname* (n. 15); see also IACtHR, *Case of the Sawoyamaxa Indigenous Community v. Paraguay*, Judgment (Merits, Reparations, and Costs), 29 March 2006.

[34] Rodríguez-Garavito, 'The Globalization of the Vernacular: Globalizing, Resisting, and Transforming International Human Rights from Below' in P. Alston (ed.), *Essays in Honor of Sally Merry* (forthcoming)

[35] On the concept of human rights vernacularization, see S. Merry, *Human Rights and Gender Violence: Translating International Law into Local Justice* (2006).

mobilization for Indigenous rights and environmental protection in the US against the construction of a major pipeline in Lakota territory. In the middle of the frigid February winter in the Lakota lands, the Sarayaku leaders conveyed the same message on FPIC, the rights of nature, and the opposition to extractive economies that they have been communicating to a global audience from the tropical forest.[36]

More recently, by replicating internationally the type of framing, direct action, and media tactics that they have fruitfully pursued at the domestic level, the Sarayaku forged bridges with the nascent global movement for climate action. As noted, one of the most striking tactics was the construction and shipping of a canoe from the Amazon to Paris, which Sarayaku leaders sailed down the Seine during the Paris climate summit in 2015. In a hummingbird-shaped canoe, a group of Sarayaku female activists demanded that world leaders take urgent measures to protect Indigenous territories and put an end to reliance on extractive industries in order to avert climate catastrophe.[37] Stepping off the canoe, Patricia Gualinga encapsulated the global reach of the Sarayaku message:

> We have to unite to fight against everything that is happening. It is time to break down the prejudices that disunite us. It is time for unity. We from the Amazon, from India, from Indonesia, from all parts of the world have to join forces and fight because the destiny and the future of the world is also part of our responsibility. We are responsible and if we leave the decisions in the hands of the governments nothing will work. We have to act now. We do not have time to say that others should do it, it is time to do it ourselves.

Four years later, just as they prepared to go back to the Constitutional Court to demand that their territory be recognized as a subject of rights, the Sarayaku's message was being integrated into the rising global youth movement for urgent climate action. At 'The Amazon, Center of the World'—a summit of Amazonian Indigenous leaders, scientists, and activists from Extinction Rebellion and #FridaysforFuture held in the Brazilian Amazon in late 2019—young climate activists issued a declaration that included a demand for the protection of FPIC and Indigenous rights.[38] Another bridge has formed with another ecological frame as a result of the Catholic Church's increasing environmental advocacy under Pope Francis.

Patricia Gualinga, once again, embodied this articulation. After being invited by the Vatican to participate in the Synod of the Bishops of the Amazon and the Pope in late 2019, she became a member of the committee responsible for implementing the Synod's conclusions. She accepted the responsibility as an opportunity to weave yet another strand in the patiently crafted network of the Sarayaku. 'We celebrate that the Church has become an ally in our defense of our territory and ecosystem', said

[36] See 'Sarayaku in Standing Rock' for a video clip on their participation in the Standing Rock protests, AmazonWatch, *Sarayaku in Standing Rock*, 27 February 2017, https://www.youtube.com/watch?v=yTEfHlNyZFM (last visited 7 December 2020).

[37] See n. 1.

[38] J. Watts, *Activists Hold Climate Conference Deep in the Amazon Rainforest*, 15 November 2019, https://www.theguardian.com/environment/2019/nov/15/a-journey-to-the-centre-of-the-amazon-in-radical-bid-to-solve-climate-crisis (last visited 7 December 2020).

Gualinga. 'And we are proud that young people are rising up around the world and are willing to be more courageous than past generations.'[39]

4. Conclusion

In this chapter, we have argued that legal mobilization should be understood not only in terms of the opportunities or obstacles that legal rules pose to activists, but also in terms of how activists use the law to frame their struggles. Put differently, the rise and outcomes of contentious legal action depend not only on opportunity structures for mobilization, but also on activists' efforts to frame their cause in ways that resonate with courts and other audiences and forges bridges with other movements.

We have illustrated the workings of framing in legal mobilization through a case study of the Sarayaku campaign and litigation against oil drilling in their territory. We have shown that the Sarayaku's success in fending off multiple attempts at oil exploitation largely hinges on their effectiveness at articulating an alternative, broader framing of FPIC as requiring Indigenous peoples' consent (as opposed to consultation) and the protection of the rights of nature and future generations. As this framing strategy has resonated with a global audience, it has influenced international law and the movements for Indigenous rights, the protection of the environment, climate action, and the rights of future generations.

The prominence of intergenerational justice in the Sarayaku struggle relates to a distinctive aspect of legal advocacy around Indigenous rights that is seldom noticed in legal mobilization studies. The continuity of the Sarayaku campaign for over a quarter of a century, as well as the long-term focus of its demands for the protection of nature and future generations, reminds us of the salience of time in this type of legal advocacy. The tactics and frames of the Indigenous and climate movements stand in contrast to the blindness to issues of time that is common in human rights research and activism. This is evident, for instance, in the neglect of the rights of future generations—a central concern in Indigenous and climate legal mobilization—in mainstream human rights concepts and norms. For instance, when the Universal Declaration of Human Rights proclaims that 'all human beings are born free and equal in dignity and rights', it considers only present generations because its provisions do not prevent them from leaving an uninhabitable planet to future generations.

The Sarayaku movement exhibits what can be called a 'long-termist' view of rights.[40] From this perspective, the 'human' in 'human rights' encompasses not only the nearly eight billion people alive today (including young people who are likely to face existential threats in this century and the next) but also the innumerable generations yet to be born. Instances of this view can be found in many other Indigenous movements—as reflected, for instance, in the seven-generations principle of the Haudenosaunee

[39] ZENIT, *Patricia Gualinga: 'Amazonizar es que, quien creía saberlo todo, re-aprenda mientras el olvidado le enseña'*, 9 January 2020, https://es.zenit.org/articles/patricia-gualinga-amazonizar-es-que-quien-creia-saberlo-todo-re-aprenda-mientras-el-olvidado-le-ensena/ (last visited 7 December 2020).

[40] C. Rodríguez-Garavito, 'Can Human Rights Deal with Existential Risks to Humanity and the Planet?', *Open Global Rights*, 22 January 2021, https://www.openglobalrights.org/the-future-of-human-rights-blog/ (last visited 17 September 2021)

Indigenous people of North America, according to which decision makers need to act in the interest not only of present generations but also of the next seven generations.

The Sarayaku's insistence on protecting the interests of future generations and the 'deep time' of the cycles of nature has stood in stark contrast with the frenetic pace of extractive economies and development programs in the Amazon and other Indigenous territories. And it will probably sustain the movement for a long time to come.

6
Critical Legal Empowerment for Human Rights

*Margaret Satterthwaite**

> You cannot defend human rights when you are 'above' and the people you are defending are 'below'. In a horizontal space, the people have information, consider it, and determine a course of action.
>
> (James Olriche Pierre, Kolektif Jistis Min, Haiti)

1. Why Legal Empowerment for Human Rights?

It has been a decade since the UN's Commission on Legal Empowerment of the Poor found that four billion people live outside the protection of the law.[1] Ten years on, the estimate has reached 5.1 billion.[2] This shocking statistic summarizes deep and broad forms of exclusion and subordination that persist today: immigrant families who are forced to live below the radar of the law rather than seeking its protection in the face of exploitative labour conditions; pregnant women who die when their local health centre is again out of needed materials for an emergency blood transfusion; and Indigenous communities that are left without recourse when a mining company's wastewater dam breaks and floods farmers' land with cyanide-laced water. Beyond formal exclusions, many communities that are formally 'protected' by the law in fact experience the legal system as a regime that actively devalues their lives, with often deadly consequences—as killings by police of Black Americans in the United States demonstrate. These are all human rights violations: they abrogate the right to equality, to be free from slavery, to enjoy fair working conditions, and to be recognized before the law; the right to healthcare, and gender equality; Indigenous rights; the rights to

* I am grateful to the South Rupununi District Council for their permission to include the case study presented in this chapter. I acknowledge with thanks the incisive comments and suggestions made on earlier drafts of this chapter by Sukti Dhital, Ellie Happel, Gráinne de Búrca, Lynnette Chua, Paula Fernandez-Wulff, Fergus MacKay, César Rodríguez-Garavito, Dorothy Estrada Tanck, and Lisa Vanhala. My appreciation goes to Chang Hahn and Julia Krusen for their research assistance. Research for this chapter was supported by the Filomen D'Agostino Research Fund at New York University School of Law.

[1] Commission on Legal Empowerment of the Poor and United Nations Development Programme, *Making the Law Work for Everyone: Report of the Commission on Legal Empowerment*, vol. 1 (2008).

[2] Task Force on Justice, *Justice for All—Final Report* 38 (2019), https://bf889554-6857-4cfe-8d55-8770007b8841.filesusr.com/ugd/90b3d6_746fc8e4f9404abeb994928d3fe85c9e.pdf (last visited 12 October 2020).

Margaret Satterthwaite, *Critical Legal Empowerment for Human Rights* In: *Legal Mobilization for Human Rights*.
Edited by: Gráinne de Búrca, Oxford University Press.
DOI: 10.1093/oso/9780192866578.003.0006

water and to a healthy environment; and the rights to equality and to life. Such violations happen every day, with justice beyond the reach of those experiencing the abuse. But what is the best way to tackle these problems? More and more, it is apparent that the old human rights methods of 'naming and shaming' are insufficient[3]—even if updated to include new narrative and interdisciplinary strategies.[4]

This chapter argues that a deep change in approach is needed to alter the basic conditions of those who experience persistent human rights violations. Legal empowerment—led by the grassroots, with lawyers and other professionals in supporting, rather than leading roles—is a crucial part of the justice transformation that is needed. When rights-holders directly engage institutions affecting their lives, they demand that systems become more accessible and responsive to the daily challenges of the people. And when the law and legal systems are actively harming marginalized and oppressed peoples, a critical form of legal empowerment can ensure they are the authors of their own liberation and demand transformation of the law. Human rights advocates should embrace this reality by becoming reliable partners to movements led by the communities experiencing grave rights deprivations.[5] Human rights advocacy should support community justice workers such as paralegals, community-based monitors, and movement organizers. They should ensure that strategic litigation is rooted in the most pressing concerns articulated by communities, collectivities, and movements. And they should take their cue in law and policy reform efforts from communities who seek to shape the law into a more accurate reflection of the justice they seek. Such transformations aim to make human rights advocates reliable allies

[3] S. Dhital, *Reimagining Justice: Human Rights Through Legal Empowerment*, 23 April 2018, https://www.openglobalrights.org/Reimagining-justice-human-rights-through-legal-empowerment/ (last visited 12 October 2020). Of course, acknowledging that these methods are insufficient does not mean they are ineffective. Reports and other campaigning materials written on the basis of interviews, testimony, and crowd-sourced materials remain crucial and can advance reform at specific moments—especially, as Kathryn Sikkink has found, 'when naming and shaming is done by networks with connections to domestic human rights NGOs in the target states'. K. Sikkink, *Evidence for Hope: Making Human Rights Work in the 21st Century* (2018) 212.

[4] For discussion of shifts in human rights fact-finding, research, and advocacy, see generally P. Alston and S. Knuckey (eds), *The Transformation of Human Rights Fact-Finding* (2016). When findings from fields such as neuroscience, social psychology, and data visualization are taken into account, human rights advocacy can become more effective: materials can be designed to inspire hope, to provide clear messages calling for change, and to overcome obstacles such as compassion fade. For a discussion of compassion fade, see Butts and Gabriel, 'Helping One or Helping Many? A Theoretical Integration and Meta-Analytic Review of the Compassion Fade Literature', 151 *Organizational Behavior & Human Decision Processes* (2019) 16 (meta-analysis of 41 studies finds that 'victim group size negatively affects both helping intent and helping behavior'). For findings on how to inspire hope in human rights contexts, see Open Global Rights, *A Guide to Hope-based Communications* (2019), https://www.openglobalrights.org/hope-guide/ (last visited 12 October 2020). For research on data visualization in human rights settings, see Rall *et al.*, 'Data Visualization for Human Rights Advocacy', 8 *Journal of Human Rights Practice* (2016) 171. See also Sikkink, 'Why Is It So Hard to Measure the Effectiveness of Human Rights?', in *Evidence for Hope* (n. 3) 139, 152–178 (discussing how the information paradox, heuristics and biases, and changing standards of accountability confound efforts to assess the effectiveness of human rights law, institutions, and movements). Perhaps most importantly, international campaigns, when artfully crafted using broad coalitions, can turn the tide when they are responsive to, and coordinated with local advocates. For a discussion of how to create such effective coalitions, see Crisis Action, *Creative Coalitions: A Handbook for Change* (2017), https://crisisaction.org/handbook/contents/ (last visited 12 October 2020).

[5] For an example of a scholarly argument along these lines, see Snyder, 'Empowering Rights through Mass Movements, Religion and Reform Parties', in S. Hopgood, J. Snyder, and L. Vinjamuri (eds), *Human Rights Futures* (2017) 94 ('I argue that the human rights movement can make substantial progress toward achieving its goals if—and only if—it does a better job tapping into the latent power of mass civil society').

in efforts to shift power towards those most directly affected. To achieve this shift, accurate terminology is also needed, to distinguish technocratic, development-focused, and sometimes top-down forms of legal empowerment from the more thoroughgoing kind, which seeks to build the power of movements to change the way societies organize themselves. In the next section, I suggest that human rights advocates should embrace a 'critical' form of legal empowerment, using insights from movement lawyering to reflect on our role in transformational work. This recommendation draws on work done by colleagues at the Bernstein Institute for Human Rights and the Global Justice Clinic at NYU School of Law and discussions with—and learning from the practice of—legal empowerment practitioners, activists, and scholars who work in this critical space.[6] I take responsibility for any missteps in setting out this concept, but to the extent these ideas are useful, I do not claim credit as their author.[7]

2. Defining Critical Legal Empowerment

Scholars have argued that the legalism of the human rights movement has been one of the major forces behind its enormous failings.[8] While many aspects of these critiques have been refuted,[9] the underlying concern retains its salience: human rights activism—especially the type concentrated in large, Northern-based NGOs—has often focused its energies on the adoption or ratification of international treaties, formal legal changes, and victories in big cases.[10] Human rights advocates have too

[6] I have learned directly from many who practice what I call here a critical form of legal empowerment, especially Sukti Dhital and Ellie Happel at NYU; Vivek Maru at Namati; Jhody Polk of LEAH; Meena Jagannath of the Movement Law Lab; Nixon Boumba of the Ensemble Contre la Corruption, Samuel Nesner of SOKIJA, and James Olriche Pierre of the Kolektif Jistis Min in Haiti; as well as from the writing, spoken words, and work of Amna Akbar of Ohio State University, Marbre Stahly-Butts of Law for Black Lives, Purvi Shah of Movement Law Lab, Ravi Ragbir of the New Sanctuary Coalition, Raj Jayadev of Silicon Valley Debug, Antonio Gutierrez of Organized Communities Against Deportation, and the organizations of the Justice Power Network, discussed below. While I attribute these activists with teaching me about the critical practice of legal empowerment, I am responsible for the errors and misunderstandings this article no doubt contains. While I offer this concept in part to lift up their work, I should note that they have not endorsed this concept.

[7] As a white cisgender lesbian American law professor, I recognize that my perspective is partial and skewed in many respects. For a discussion of the importance of reflexivity in legal scholarship, see Harris, 'Racing Law: Legal Scholarship and the Critical Race Revolution', 52 *Equity & Excellence in Education* (2019) 12, at 17–18. I am especially grateful to those who have provided input into earlier drafts of this chapter for pointing out shortcomings and misperceptions, including Sukti Dhital, Ellie Happel, Fergus MacKay, Paula Fernandez-Wulff, and Gráinne de Búrca.

[8] Snyder and Vinjamuri, 'Trials and Errors: Principle and Pragmatism in Strategies of International Justice', 28 *International Security* (2003) 5; J. Goldsmith and E. Posner, *The Limits of International Law* (2005); E. Posner, *The Perils of Global Legalism* (2009); S. Moyn, *The Last Utopia: Human Rights in History* (2010); S. Hopgood, *The Endtimes of Human Rights* (2013); E. Posner, *The Twilight of Human Rights Law* (2014).

[9] See e.g. Dancy and Fariss, 'Rescuing Human Rights Law from International Legalism and its Critics', 39 *Human Rights Quarterly* (2017) 1 (arguing that the critiques of human rights legalism use an outdated realist model of the law that does not account for the very real changes that human rights law, activism, and politics have helped create).

[10] Hafner-Burton and Ron, 'Review: Seeing Double: Human Rights Impact through Qualitative and Quantitative Eyes', 61 *World Politics* (2011) 360 (reviewing *Human Rights and Structural Adjustment* by M. Abouharb and D. Cingranelli; *The Marketing of Rebellion: Insurgents, Media, and International Activism* by C. Bob; *Conflict and Compliance: State Responses to International Human Rights Pressure* by

often been 'elite, professionalized shamers and blamers documenting failures to comply with international law'.[11] This orientation has been to the detriment of other methods for ensuring behavioural change in government institutions, business practices, and international organizations of the type that would transform peoples' daily lives. In many ways, human rights advocacy has often empowered lawyers more than communities.

However, in many places around the world, another model is being pursued. The monopoly that lawyers have had on the legal system and the fight for rights is being challenged from the bottom up: community paralegals and 'barefoot lawyers' are working with people to pursue their own claims; community-based monitors are uncovering rights violations at the grassroots level; and strategic litigation is being driven by movements themselves, used as a tool for broader mobilization and institutional change. From a human rights perspective, the promise of these approaches lies not only in their efficacy, but also in the way they advance what rights-based approaches have demanded of government officials but not always of themselves. They require that lawyers recognize—and follow—the leadership of those who are the targets of injustice; they demand the accountability of lawyers to rights-holders; and they require engagement with community demands for equality as rights claims—whether supported by the existing law or not.[12] Further, legal empowerment strategies facilitate the broad 'localization'[13] and 'vernacularization' of human rights,[14] as they involve people advancing and claiming their own rights in their own idiom. Legal empowerment also enlarges the focus on actors impacting human rights, engaging not only the usual (national) suspects but also frontline state agents like local police officers or doctors and nurses in medical outposts, as well as non-state actors—from the local to the global—that exercise significant power over communities, including representatives of companies or development NGOs.[15] Indeed, in many contexts, legal empowerment suggests a shift away from dichotomies such as state v. private sector or

S. Cardenas; *Unexpected Power: Conflict and Change among Transnational Activists* by S. Hertel; *Keepers of the Flame: Understanding Amnesty International* by S. Hopgood; *Protecting Human Rights: A Comparative Study* by T. Landman; *Human Rights and Gender Violence: Translating International Law into Local Justice* by S. Merry; *Torture and Democracy* by D. Rejali).

[11] Snyder, 'Empowering Rights through Mass Movements, Religion and Reform Parties', in S. Hopgood, J. Snyder, and L. Vinjamuri (eds), *Human Rights Futures* (2017) 89.

[12] Knuckey and Satterthwaite, 'Should Human Rights Practice be Rights-Based?', in N. Bhuta *et al.*, *The Struggle for Human Rights: Essays in Honour of Philip Alston* (2021); Satterthwaite and Klasing, 'A Rights-Based Approach to Research: Assessing the Right to Water in Haiti', in E. Beracochea *et al.*, *Rights-Based Approaches to Public Health* (2011) 143; S. Knuckey, A. Parrin, and L. Fondebrider, *Human Rights-Based Forensic Anthropology and Mass Killing Investigations in Low Resource Settings: From Theory to Practice* (forthcoming).

[13] Mattingly, *Thirteen Insights from the Front Lines of Human Rights Activism*, 13 December 2019 ('Grassroots activists are the people best placed to solve the problems facing their communities . . . it is much more effective to invest in community-driven social change than to impose an agenda').

[14] Merry, 'Transnational Human Rights and Local Activism: Mapping the Middle', 108 *American Anthropologist* (2006) 38.

[15] For example, see Nesner and Happel, *In Haiti, Legal Empowerment Is Resistance Against Exploitation*, 27 August 2018, https://www.openglobalrights.org/in-haiti-legal-empowerment-is-resistance-against-exploitation/ (last visited 12 October 2020) ('Haitian communities are building their power, and making demands not only of the government, but of other relevant actors—for example, companies and international financial institutions').

local v. international and towards more embedded understandings of how power plays itself out across borders and in given contexts. Legal empowerment centres and demands accountability from all powerful actors impacting the human rights of the disempowered.[16]

A focus on how communities and movements are using legal empowerment to address the daily impacts of global injustice is similar to how Santos and Rodríguez-Garavito have used the lens of 'subaltern cosmopolitanism'.[17] A 'bottom-up approach to the study of law in globalization', subaltern cosmopolitanism focuses on 'detailed case studies of counter-hegemonic legal forms', with the aim of advancing those forms, 'reconnecting law and politics and reimagining legal institutions from below'.[18] A recent review of the literature of subaltern cosmopolitanism suggests that the concept does not cohere around a unified theory, but instead 'has helped scholars theorize [the] social and political agency of a wide range of peripheral subjectivities and broaden the possibilities of resistance and empowerment against hegemony of various kinds'.[19]

I suggest that a focus on legal empowerment—as a practice, an approach, and a lens—may allow scholars of human rights to broaden our understanding of how communities and movements are engaging with the law and legal systems to advance their human rights and to resist exclusion and oppression. Further, categorizing these efforts under the rubric of legal empowerment may allow us to see the cross-movement ways that practitioners are building 'new forms of connectivity, solidarity and interactions of globalization'[20] out of the commonalities of their legally inflected struggles. Indeed, there are powerful nodes of learning, solidarity, and support forming around the concept of legal empowerment. The Global Legal Empowerment Network, led by the legal empowerment organization Namati:

> brings together 2154 organizations and 7887 individuals, all dedicated to grassroots justice. We meet online and in-person. We learn from each other and share a growing library of legal empowerment resources. We campaign on issues that affect us globally and nationally. We work together to secure support and sustainable funding for our field.[21]

However, this chapter suggests that the potential of legal empowerment will be more fully realized when it embraces what movement lawyers have long recommended: a 'critical' shift to understanding that social change—and transformations

[16] See e.g. Purkey, 'A Dignified Approach: Legal Empowerment and Justice for Human Rights Violations in Protracted Refugee Situations', 27 *Journal of Refugee Studies* (2014) 260, at 261, https://doi.org/10.1093/jrs/fet031 (last visited 12 October 2020) (describing legal empowerment as a means 'to enhance the accountability of powerful actors for the protection and fulfilment of refugee and community rights').

[17] B. de Sousa Santos and C. Rodríguez-Garavito, *Law and Globalization from Below: Towards a Cosmopolitan Legality* (2005) 15.

[18] See n. 17. This approach is in line with Upendra Baxi's efforts to ensure that human rights are authored not by 'the politics of intergovernmental desire' but by 'the multitudinous struggles of people against human violation'. U. Baxi, *The Future of Human Rights* (3rd Indian ed., 2008) 263.

[19] Zeng, 'Subaltern Cosmopolitanism: Concept and Approaches', 62 *Sociological Review* (2014) 137, at 140.

[20] Wilson, 'Discoursing on Slums: Representing the Cosmopolitan Subaltern', in P. K. Malreddy *et al.* (eds), *Reworking Postcolonialism* (2015) 229, at 231.

[21] Namati, *About the Network*, https://namati.org/network/ (last visited 12 October 2020).

in major economic, social, and cultural structures—will come only when legal efforts effectively build the power of communities facing human rights violations to transform those systems.[22] Building political power and armed with legal tools, movements can change the conditions of communities by shifting power within societies for good. Such political power is also needed to change the global systems that have led to radical inequality in their results. At a time when those results—including racialized mortality and the death of working class 'frontline workers' in global pandemics and the deathly injustice of climate change's unfolding disasters—are front and centre, human rights has an opportunity to join with internationally aware and globally inflected movements, embracing legal empowerment and other methods for transformation, renewing the spirit of a field that has become increasingly irrelevant in many places.

This 'critical' component of critical legal empowerment entails a rejection of the technocratic approaches sometimes forwarded by access to justice practitioners and an embrace of community-based efforts to engage the legal system in strategies to shift power downward. Inspired by scholars of critical race theory, this quality of critique also requires self-reflection, humility, and a commitment to critical praxis—a groundedness in the grassroots.[23]

This chapter highlights some of the main strategies being used by legal empowerment practitioners, with examples from a variety of contexts that demonstrate how critical forms of empowerment are being embraced. The use of community paralegals, community-based monitoring, strategic litigation, and accompaniment will be considered, and an in-depth case study concerning the deployment of law from below will be presented.[24] The goal of this chapter is both descriptive and normative: to introduce legal empowerment to human rights practitioners, to suggest and define the term 'critical legal empowerment', and to demonstrate that these approaches are being used to sometimes remarkable effect. I also argue that the invitation to engage with legal empowerment offers much to human rights in its much-discussed time of crisis. Indeed, the attention to critical legal empowerment can help us decolonize the concept of a 'failing' international human rights project by opening our eyes to ways dispossessed communities in many places are advancing their own rights, often effectively, if also frequently outside the gaze of (dominant-group, academic) international human rights scholars and practitioners.[25] The next section will examine the concept

[22] For an excellent compilation of readings on movement lawyering, see *The Movement Lawyering Reading Guide* developed by Purvi Shah, https://static1.squarespace.com/static/5500a55ae4b05a69b3350e23/t/57802cbd893fc04f8168473a/1468017897029/Movement+Lawyering+Reading+Guide (last visited 12 October 2020).

[23] See Harris (n. 7); Yamamoto, 'Critical Race Praxis: Race Theory and Political Lawyering Practice in Post-Civil Rights America', 95 *Michigan Law Review* (1997) 821, at 873–880 (calling for a 'critical race praxis', defined as 'combines critical pragmatic socio-legal analysis with political lawyering and community organizing for justice practice by and for racialized communities. Its central idea is racial justice as antisubordination practice', with the praxis a way of 'infusing antiracism practice with aspects of critical inquiry and pragmatism, and then recasting theory in light of practical experience').

[24] The case study examines the work of a community with which my clinic at NYU has partnered. The information in the case study is based on publicly available information authored by, or approved by, community structures. No privileged or confidential information is included in this chapter, and the community's governing structure has reviewed and agreed to the publication of the case study.

[25] In this way, the chapter places itself in conversation with other similar efforts. See e.g. K. Grewal, *The Socio-Political Practice of Human Rights: Between the Universal and the Particular* (2016).

of legal empowerment and suggest ways it could be broadened to embrace the critical practices that communities and movements are using to resist structural oppression and transform systems.

A. From Legal Empowerment of the Poor to Critical Legal Empowerment

Communities have embraced legal empowerment practices—such as the use of community paralegals—for many decades. Vivek Maru and Varun Gauri explain that South African organizers deployed community paralegals in work to resist apartheid as early as the 1950s.[26] By the early 2000s, major development agencies, including the World Bank, the Asian Development Bank, and the Carnegie Endowment had embraced some version of 'legal empowerment' as a method of combatting poverty.[27] Rejecting 'rule of law' orthodoxies that focused on formal legal institutions, the term 'legal empowerment' was commonly used to denote the recognition and formalization of claims on the state made by people living in poverty.[28] Described variously as a way of combating poverty and enhancing the agency of the poor by bringing the informal sector into the fold of the recognized economy, the substantive focus was often on 'the formalization of property rights, or the simplification of business regulations, or the reform of the justice system'.[29] This coupling of property, business, and justice system reform is significant. It placed the emphasis of legal empowerment on a process aimed at bringing those who were still unincorporated in the global capitalist order—including Indigenous Peoples, smallholder farmers, and slum dwellers—into the fold of the neoliberal state.

The concept was broadly popularized when it was taken up by the Commission on Legal Empowerment of the Poor, which reported in 2008 that four million people are 'robbed of the chance to better their lives and climb out of poverty, because they are excluded from the rule of law'.[30] The Commission defined legal empowerment as:

> the process through which the poor become protected and are enabled to use the law to advance their rights and their interests … It involves the poor realising their full rights, and reaping the opportunities that flow from that, through public support and their own efforts as well as the efforts of their supporters and wider networks. Legal empowerment is a country and context-based approach that takes place at both the national and local levels.[31]

[26] Maru and Gauri, 'Paralegals in Comparative Perspective', in V. Maru and V. Gauri (eds), *Community Paralegals and the Pursuit of Justice* (2018) 4.

[27] See World Bank, *Legal Empowerment of the Poor: An Action Agenda for the World Bank*, at 15–16 (2006), http://documents.worldbank.org/curated/en/991871468331228461/Legal-empowerment-of-the-poor-an-action-agenda-for-the-World-Bank (last visited 12 October 2020).

[28] Golub, 'Beyond Rule of Law Orthodoxy: The Legal Empowerment Alternative', *Carnegie Endowment for International Peace Working Papers* 41 (October 2003) 3, 33–37.

[29] World Bank (n. 27).

[30] Commission on Legal Empowerment of the Poor and United Nations Development Programme, *Making the Law Work for Everyone: Report of the Commission on Legal Empowerment*, vol. 1 (2008).

[31] Ibid. 26.

In the dozen years following publication of the Commission's report, the idea of legal empowerment has matured, expanded, and infused efforts to extend access to justice carried out by development agencies, governments, and NGOs. Many practitioners have argued that legal empowerment as deployed by development agencies has been too focused on simple 'inclusion' in the formal processes of law, leading to the reification of existing power relations.[32] In a recent article, Gisselquist explains that there are 'narrow' and 'broad' concepts of legal empowerment, with the former focusing on formal rights within given legal and economic systems and the latter engaged with efforts to use law and legal systems to more fully transform the lives of the poor. [33] This approach is aligned with what Hopgood has labelled 'human rights'—a bottom-up endeavour to change society and politics, in counter-distinction to 'Human Rights'—a top-down agenda for change.[34] For those who practice in and study in this 'broader' or bottom-up version of the field, legal empowerment is a method of advancing access to justice that aims to 'increase disadvantaged populations' control over their lives'[35] by capacitating communities to make claims of—and to change—the systems impacting their quest for justice and equality. While these claims are sometimes backed by formal law, there are many contexts where claims by marginalized communities have been ignored or left out of the law. In these contexts, legal empowerment will require major changes in the law and legal institutions.

As Joshi has explained, numerous tools are relied upon in such legal empowerment efforts, but they usually encompass legal awareness-raising, provision of legal services, dispute resolution, and law reform.[36] Thus, while there are many pathways to legal empowerment, the broad, 'bottom-up', human rights–focused ones are aimed at enabling people to 'know, use, and shape the law', bringing about transformations in 'knowledge, agency, and governance'.[37] In addition, as Waldorf explains, this approach to legal empowerment 'emphasises rights, participation, and accountability ... [I]t adopts a pragmatic approach to legal pluralism, working with formal, customary, and religious law'.[38] The 'empowerment' sought is the critical agency to analyse reality from the perspective of the oppressed and to make change: 'social transformation—not only a more just distribution of wealth and income, but a more expansive sharing

[32] For example, Bård A. Andreassen argues that the embrace of legal formalities—especially the right to property—should be corrected through infusion of human rights approaches in legal empowerment efforts. See 'The Right to Development and Legal Empowerment of the Poor', 33 *Bangladesh Development Studies* (2010) 311, www.jstor.org/stable/23339890 (last visited 12 October 2020).

[33] Gisselquist, 'Legal Empowerment and Group-Based Inequality', 55 *Journal of Development Studies* (2019) 333, at 336, DOI: 10.1080/00220388.2018.1451636.

[34] Hopgood (n. 8)

[35] Joshi, 'Legal Empowerment and Social Accountability: Complementary Strategies Toward Rights-based Development in Health?', 99 *World Development* (2017) 160, at 162 (quoting and citing Golub).

[36] Ibid. 163 (note that Joshi includes litigation as a separate category; I have included it in the provision of legal services).

[37] Maru and Manuel, *Session I: Conceptual Framework – Introduction to Legal Empowerment*, 1 December 2019, https://community.namati.org/t/lelc-2019-legal-empowerment-community-organizing-sessions-day-1/71079 (last visited 12 October 2020).

[38] Waldorf, 'Introduction: Legal Empowerment in Transitions', 3 *International Journal of Human Rights* (2015) 229. Perhaps most importantly, Waldorf believes that '[l]egal empowerment contains an inherent, normative assumption that law is empowering rather than disempowering'. I would suggest that the normative belief is instead that law *can be made to be* empowering—often through bottom-up efforts to shape, reform, or reorient the law.

of power' that enables disempowered people to make 'significant change through their own actions'.[39] As legal empowerment is normatively rooted in human rights law, these changes advance the rights of those disempowered within existing systems.[40]

This chapter will provide examples of such efforts. However, it also focuses its attention on contexts where the law has itself been a central tool in defining, crushing, and dispossessing marginalized communities. In such settings, legal empowerment cannot only seek the *inclusion* of marginalized communities and the *reform* of existing law. Instead, it must seek thoroughgoing change in the aims of legal systems. Achieving such changes requires movement building, organizing, and coalition work. It demands a reconceptualization of what the law is, what it can do, and *who* it can do those things for. It also demands what Gerald López calls 'rebellious lawyering',[41] in which self-reflection, humility,[42] and critical inquiry are essential for those who see themselves as legal professionals aligned with communities. For these reasons, and based on critiques coming from scholars and communities in the United States, I suggest the term 'critical legal empowerment' to highlight how communities are engaging critically with the law as a form of power and partnering with lawyers who know their (limited) place in these struggles. Critical legal empowerment requires a careful examination of where law and justice collide, and an effort to ensure that law bends towards justice and away from oppression. It also requires an embrace of movement direction and ownership. In this sense, critical legal empowerment is aimed not only at ensuring people can know, use, and shape the law, but they can also transform legal systems.

As feminists—especially feminists of colour and those based in the Global South[43]—have argued, when the 'power' in 'empowerment' is emphasized and interrogated from an intersectional angle, 'empowerment is simultaneously an instrument for social transformation and an end in and of itself'.[44] This 'liberating' form of empowerment is the one being employed in what I am calling critical legal empowerment efforts. It is bound up with efforts to change major systems of oppression and domination, which require organized movements[45] and not only NGO or government 'projects' or 'initiatives'. In this way, critical legal empowerment is inspired by what has been called movement lawyering in the United States, defined as:

> the mobilization of law through deliberately planned and interconnected advocacy strategies, inside and outside of formal law-making spaces, by lawyers who are

[39] n.1 281.

[40] Gisselquist, 'Legal Empowerment and Group-Based Inequality', 55 *Journal of Development Studies* (2019) 333, at 336, DOI: 10.1080/00220388.2018.1451636.

[41] G. López, *Rebellious Lawyering: One Chicano's Vision of Progressive Law Practice* (1992).

[42] Hung, 'Movement Lawyering as Rebellious Lawyering: Advocating with Humility, Love and Courage', 23 *Clinical Law Review* (2017) 663, at 665; Kassem and Shamas, 'Rebellious Lawyering in the Security State', 23 *Clinical Law Review* (2017) 671, at 704.

[43] I use the term 'Global South' to denote spaces 'historically conquered or controlled by modern imperial powers, leaving a continuing legacy of poverty, economic exploitation and dependence'. See Meekosha, 'Decolonizing Disability: Thinking and Acting Globally', 26 *Disability and Society* (2011) 667.

[44] C. Sardenberg, *Liberal vs. Liberating Empowerment: Conceptualising Empowerment from a Latin American Feminist Perspective* (2008), https://assets.publishing.service.gov.uk/media/57a08b6c40f0b6497 4000b3e/PathwaysWP7-website.pdf (last visited 12 October 2020) (citing Batliwala, defining 'liberating empowerment' in distinction to 'liberal empowerment' used in development discourses).

[45] Ibid.

> accountable to politically marginalized constituencies to build the power of those constituencies to produce and sustain democratic social change goals that they define.[46]

As Guinier and Torres explain, movement lawyering involves a 'participatory, power-sharing process within the lawyer/client relationship', between lawyers and marginalized groups, aimed at contributing to the 'cultural shifts that make durable legal change possible'.[47] While movement lawyering focuses on the role of the lawyer in social movements and insists that the 'lawyer is not the protagonist',[48] critical legal empowerment focuses on how communities engage with the law directly—sometimes in partnership with lawyers and sometimes on their own. In this way, it is both a practice and a lens, making visible the work communities and movements are doing to transform legal systems.

Although critical legal empowerment efforts exceed any specific project or organization, they embrace existing legal empowerment tools, adding others where these are inadequate and redefining the existing ones to emphasize collective power. Common models for legal empowerment include the deployment of paralegals or 'barefoot lawyers', community-based monitoring of rights and institutions, engaging with community-based dispute resolution, and strategic litigation aimed at ending structural injustice. Critical approaches add to this inventory by including new tools and infusing existing approaches with a power-building ethos. For example, the Justice Power Network based at the Bernstein Institute in the United States uplifts legal empowerment programmes that advance the rights of asylum seekers, refugees, and immigrants in the US using both traditional legal empowerment tools and innovative strategies.[49] These strategies were developed specifically to advance the rights of those rendered by US law as 'rightsless'—communities described as 'undocumented' or even 'illegal' but imbued with human rights and claims for justice that reject these dehumanizing and criminalizing descriptions. The strategies these communities have developed include the use of accompaniment, community paralegals, conveners, community driven campaigns and litigation, hotlines, pro se legal clinics, and tech innovation.[50] As Claudia Muñoz of Grassroots Leadership explains, 'We know and believe that the people that can transform the systems are the people that have been through these systems. Nobody has better answers, nobody has more urgency.'[51] The next section of this chapter will discuss the spectrum of legal empowerment tools—including several overtly 'critical' tools—in the hopes of lifting up critical legal empowerment as a means of mobilization for human rights that can fundamentally alter unjust systems.

[46] Cummings, 'Movement Lawyering', *University Illinois Law Review* (2017) 1645, at 1660.

[47] Ibid. (quoting and citing Guinier and Torres, 'Changing the Wind: Notes Toward a Demosprudence of Law and Social Movements', 123 *Yale Law Journal* (2014) 2740, at 2743, 2753).

[48] Gordon, 'The Lawyer Is Not the Protagonist: Community Campaigns, Law, and Social Change', 95 *California Law Review* (2007) 2133.

[49] Walton, *Legal Empowerment during COVID-19—From Justice Power to #FreeThemAll*, 20 May 2020, https://www.law.nyu.edu/centers/bernstein-institute/legal_empowerment/blogs (last visited 12 October 2020).

[50] Justice Power Network, https://justicepower.org/ (last visited 12 October 2020).

[51] Claudia Muñoz, interviewed in Justice Power Network video, 'Accompaniment', https://justicepower.org/accompaniment/ (last visited 12 October 2020).

3. Critical Legal Empowerment Approaches: Community Paralegals, Community-Based Monitoring, Strategic Litigation, and the Use of Accompaniment to Build Grassroots Power

A. Community-Based Justice Workers

Community-based justice workers—variously called community paralegals, barefoot lawyers, and legal navigators—'transfer power from the usual gatekeepers of the law—lawyers, judges, police, and state officials to ordinary people'.[52] They do this by reframing justice problems as rights claims, accompanying people in advancing such claims—approaching legal problems nimbly, reaching for the most appropriate tool in any given circumstance—and working to reshape the law in the image of justice. In the first book-length study of community paralegals, Vivek Maru and Varun Gauri analogize the role of community paralegals to that of community health workers, the force multipliers of the public health world:

> Like community health workers—who have an established place in health care delivery systems across the world—community paralegals are close to the communities in which they work and deploy a flexible set of tools. Also like community health workers, paralegals work in tandem with a strong, typically well-organized profession. While community health workers refer difficult cases to doctors and the formal medical system, community paralegals are typically connected to lawyers who can engage in litigation or high-level advocacy if the paralegals' frontline methods fail.[53]

Summarizing the findings of studies in six countries, Maru and Gauri found that paralegals use six expansive approaches in their work: education, mediation, organizing, advocacy, monitoring, and litigation (in partnership with lawyers).[54] These activities are familiar to human rights advocates, but the insistence that these tools be used in a way that is firmly community-based is a crucial imperative often missing in Human Rights efforts. For example, while human rights education (HRE) is a common rights-advancing activity, what may be a shift is legal empowerment's insistence that such education be led by community members themselves, and be aimed at building a bridge between existing community understandings and formal rights claims rather than the other way around. These imperatives could help ensure that HRE is aimed at identifying and fostering the 'sense of entitlement'[55] that communities crushed by injustice already have, linking that felt awareness with knowledge of the law, thereby helping people shift from experiencing 'needs' to asserting demands.[56] Paralegals

[52] See n. 35.

[53] See n. 26, 3.

[54] Ibid. 10.

[55] Petchesky and Judd, 'Introduction', *Negotiating Reproductive Rights: Women's Perspectives Across Countries and Cultures* (1998) 12 (through the notion of 'sense of entitlement', the authors sought to 'illuminate the subjective component of rights (what women *feel* entitled to)', allowing examination of 'when, where, and under what circumstances does such a sense of entitlement emerge'?).

[56] Maru and Gauri (n. 26) citing Hannah Pitkin, describe this as a 'transformation of outlook' from '"I want" to "I am entitled to"'. See n. 26, 2 (quoting and citing Pitkin, 'Justice: On Relating Public and Private', 9

in Kenya, for example, work to 'improve rights consciousness', instead of imparting 'know your rights' trainings.[57] Partnering with the Global Justice Clinic, 'animators' in Haiti's mining justice movement work with communities to articulate demands concerning company actions using human rights law.[58]

Similarly, monitoring, organizing, and advocacy are familiar for human rights advocates but will have a different hue if advocates see their role as facilitating communities' own use of these tools instead of conceptualizing these as tools to be used—or led—by professionals. Mediation is a less familiar tool for many human rights workers, and its inclusion here may be challenging for those who see rights advocacy as advancing specific claims at all costs instead of seeking practical solutions to real-time problems in ways that may feel less than entirely just. Still, when conducted with rights claims in hand, mediation can be used in a way that 'enlarge[s] ... the shadow of the law' to obtain outcomes that satisfy those advancing their own claims.[59]

For example, in Mozambique, grassroots health advocates are trained by Namati to work as community justice workers in the health system.[60] This means they work with communities to understand how their sense of entitlement concerning healthcare is supported under the law, accompany them in filing grievances when those entitlements are not fulfilled, and use case data to monitor changes in the health system more broadly. Mozambique has adopted a human rights–based Charter on Patients' Rights and Obligations (*Carta dos Direitos e Deveres dos Utentes*), as well as an extensive body of laws, policies, and clinical protocols that centre the patient and give them the right to complain and receive a response from healthcare personnel. Despite the possibility for antagonism between paralegals and institutions in this setting:

> *Defensores de saúde* work to address th[e] gap between policy and reality by supporting communities in exercising their basic rights to health. They present themselves not as watchdogs who would police health care providers but rather as supporters of the system and its staff, many of whom themselves do not have access to the resources or essential information they need to work effectively. [They] share the same fundamental goal as the government: to improve health outcomes in Mozambique. This framing has been critical in building constructive relationships with both health care providers and Ministry of Health leadership.[61]

Political Theory (1981) 347). Gauri and Brinks have also characterized this shift as 'the mobilization of wants and desires into demands' in V. Gauri and D.M. Brinks, *Courting Social Justice: Judicial Enforcement of Social and Economic Rights in the Developing World* (2008) 14.

[57] Moy, 'Kenya's Community-Based Paralegals: A Tradition of Grassroots Legal Activism', in Maru and Gauri (n. 26) 180.

[58] Nesner and Happel (n. 15) and Satterthwaite, *In a World of Radical Inequality, Solidarity Is a Cornerstone of Justice*, 13 February 2020, https://www.openglobalrights.org/in-a-world-of-radical-inequality-solidarity-is-a-cornerstone-of-justice/ (last visited 12 October 2020).

[59] See n. 26, 12 (quoting and citing Berenschot and Rinaldi, 'Paralegalism in Indonesia: Balancing Relationships in the Shadow of the Law').

[60] Feinglass, Gomes, and Maru, 'Transforming Policy into Justice: The Role of Health Advocates in Mozambique', 18 *Health and Human Rights Journal* (2016) 233.

[61] Ibid.

This framing has allowed health advocates to sit down with health facility personnel to address specific grievances in a cooperative manner. For example, when HIV-positive patients were having trouble obtaining crucial test results, the *defensores de saúde* led a meeting between affected patients and the director of the health centre. Together, they brainstormed a solution that involved some immediate—but limited—improvements that the director could implement. In addition, the patients and director also agreed on joint advocacy they could undertake to higher-placed health officials for resources that would solve the problem for the long term. This kind of mediation, conducted in the enlarged 'shadow of the law', can be more effective than traditional oppositional human rights approaches. Further, it may often be more fair, since rights violations frequently come about due to systems beyond the control of frontline state actors like doctors and nurses at state-owned hospitals or medical posts.[62] As Alicia Yamin has explained, a focus on punitive measures in individual cases do not address these systemic problems and may make the human rights approach counterproductive in some health contexts.[63] This is not to say that the celebrated role of litigation in human rights movements is not applicable to the right to health. On the contrary, right to health cases have driven justice efforts forward in many places. As will be explored below, the idea here is that community justice workers are often in the ideal position to sift between claims that are best suited for mediation or community monitoring and those that are ripe for judicial determination. They can also identify well-positioned plaintiffs, understand the risks and benefits for community members in engaging in litigation, and ensure implementation of judgments following strategic wins. Community justice workers can help communities ensure that formal legal victories translate into actual change on the ground by using additional legal empowerment tools like the ones explored in the next section of this chapter.

In a more critical mode, immigrant rights organizations in the United States have begun to train and deploy community paralegals through:

> programs [that] help immigrants navigate a complicated system by empowering individuals to know and use existing laws and policies to fight for their right to remain. For example, organizations employ 'community navigators', individuals who live and work in neighborhoods with high immigrant populations who serve as legal first responders, assessing the immigration needs of those in their community, providing key information—all the more essential as immigration law and policy continues to change—and connecting immigrants with legal and social services.[64]

Immigrant rights organizations in the United States see the use of paralegals as an 'emerging' practice inside a system that resists many of the basic rights immigrant communities seek.[65] By ensuring such efforts are situated within movements and not

[62] Schaaf *et al.*, '"We All Have the Same Right to Have Health Services": A Case Study of Namati's Legal Empowerment Program in Mozambique', 20 *BMC Public Health* (2020) 1084.

[63] Yamin, 'Beyond Compassion: The Central Role of Accountability in Applying a Human Rights Framework to Health', 10 *Health & Human Rights* (2008) 1, at 4.

[64] Justice Power Network, *Community Paralegals*, https://justicepower.org/community-paralegals/ (last visited 12 October 2020).

[65] Ibid.

only inside service provision agencies, these critical practices both help individuals face the immigration system with support and contribute to shifting power to the grassroots, where efforts to transform the legal rules that define communities as 'illegal' are based.

B. Community-Based Monitoring, Groundtruthing, and Advocacy

When community members monitor the fulfilment, abrogation, and violation of their own rights, monitoring transcends simple reporting and becomes a rights-enhancing intervention of its own. By identifying injustices, collecting evidence relevant to make out claims, and directly engaging the institutions responsible for these violations, communities can instigate change in regulatory agencies, service providers, and even private sector actors such as corporations. In some situations, monitoring is a specific, targeted activity and part of the process of building community power.

For example, the human rights organization Nazdeek, which works in India, partnered with three organizations in informal settlements in Delhi to create a monitoring programme aimed at advancing core social and economic rights.[66] The organizations, dedicated to defending the rights of the Dalit and Adivasi (Indigenous Peoples) communities in which where they were based, chose women from their constituencies to be trained as paralegals. Nazdeek worked with the paralegals to identify legally guaranteed entitlements related to the rights to healthcare, food, water, and sanitation, such as the right to obtain antenatal care, receive food rations, and have garbage collected.[67] They then co-developed simple codes denoting the presence or absence of these goods and services, which were used by paralegals who visited health centres, ration shops, and communities to monitor the fulfilment of rights.[68] Using these codes, paralegals sent reports by smartphone to the Nazdeek office, where the data were collected and reported back to the community. The paralegals then used the data to advance rights claims through advocacy meetings with officials and filing grievances.

> Armed with the data reported through the platform, paralegals led a number of efforts to address the issues that emerged. They worked with affected community members to address their grievances through in-person advocacy with local government officials or by using complaint mechanisms formally set up by different government departments.[69]

The results were remarkable: all the complaints reported by the paralegals within the time period covered by a report on the programme were resolved within a month.[70]

[66] Nazdeek, *Women Lead the Way: Monitoring and Improving Government Services and Facilities in Delhi* (2018), https://indd.adobe.com/view/24c15fa2-2e91-46cc-b6ec-01e67c6c715b (last visited 12 October 2020).

[67] Ibid.

[68] Ibid. 8.

[69] Ibid. 24.

[70] Ibid. 38.

While the results were not always satisfactory, this rate of resolution is impressive and demonstrates the value of communities directly 'knowing' and 'using' the law.

In addition to these paralegal-led efforts, professional staff at Nazdeek amplified the complaints by publishing a report analysing the monitoring data and making recommendations for systemic changes to ensure rights fulfilment.[71] This report, aimed at 'shaping' the law in favour of the community, looks a lot like a traditional human rights report in format and presentation, but the facts it contains were all gathered by community justice workers, and the recommendations it forwards were based directly on lessons drawn from community monitoring and engagement with the relevant government agencies. This fidelity to community experience makes recommendations drawn from legal empowerment organizations especially valuable—and especially valid. Indeed, community monitoring and complaints function as real-world performance monitoring of government institutions meant to serve the poor and marginalized.

In another part of India, the Centre for Policy Research-Namati (CPR-N) is using legal empowerment methods to accompany communities fighting environmental injustice. For example, following years of complaints by villagers near a coal mine owned by Mahanadi Coalfields Limited in the Sundargarh district of Odisha, a number of organizations joined together to create a 'community-led "groundtruthing process"' to identify, assess, and fight the negative impacts of the mine.[72] First, the community identified its priority concerns: excessive dust, spontaneous and continuous fire in overburden dumps, and water pollution. Next, community representatives were designated for training in preparation for the groundtruthing process. CPR-N and its partners then shared information about relevant laws, standards, and conditions the company had agreed to in exchange for permission to operate the mine. Where information was missing, CPR-N and its partners provided support to the community representatives to file requests with administrative agencies using India's Right to Information (RTI) law. With the legal framework in view, the community representatives designed the groundtruthing process,[73] collecting primary and secondary data related to the priority concerns that could be used as evidence of violations of the clearance conditions placed on the company, regulations, or laws. Community representatives took photographs, collected media articles, and obtained copies of Monitoring and Compliance Reports concerning the mine through RTI applications.

[71] Ibid.

[72] Along with Namati, the Centre for Integrated Rural and Tribal Development and Hemgir Adivasi Ekta Manch have joined forces to support the community in this process. See Centre for Integrated, Rural and Tribal Development, and Centre for Policy Research-Namati Environmental Justice Program, *Closing the Enforcement Gap: Groundtruthing of Environmental Violations in Sundargarh, Odisha* (2018) 5, https://www.cprindia.org/research/reports/closing-enforcement-gap-groundtruthing-environmental-violations-sundargarh-odisha. Unless otherwise noted, all facts concerning this example were drawn from this report.

[73] Groundtruthing has been defined by Namati as 'a method through which facts stated in official documents are compared with the ground realities of a place. Through the legal empowerment approach of groundtruthing, affected people are trained to gather evidence and pursue remedies from administrative authorities who are responsible for monitoring of environmental regulation.' Dinesh, *Can Legal Compliance Address Environmental Injustice?*, March 2018, https://community.namati.org/t/can-legal-compliance-address-environmental-injustice/42111 (last visited 12 October 2020).

With these data in hand, the representatives drafted complaints alleging violations, backed by evidence. They filed these complaints with the Odisha State Pollution Control Board and the regional office of the Ministry of Environment, Forest, and Climate Change. These complaint letters sought action by the agencies to remedy the community's priority concerns. Less than one year after the complaints were filed, remedial measures had been initiated to respond to the complaints concerning two of the three priority concerns: excessive dust and spontaneous fire in overburden dumps. The community was still awaiting a response to the complaints concerning water pollution, but by January 2020, CPR-N reported that several steps had been taken to address this issue.[74] While the results are perhaps not as impressive as those reported by Nazdeek, they nonetheless represent a dramatic improvement over conditions preceding the groundtruthing exercise, since years of complaints by community members had failed to spur remedial action.[75] Further, 'rigorous follow ups' by the community continue.[76]

Critical use of community-based monitoring and advocacy aimed at transforming legal systems will be examined in the case study presented in Section 4.[77]

C. Strategic and Community-Based Litigation to End Structural Injustice

Strategic litigation plays a central role in many human rights struggles, but it has also been critiqued as being a tool of the elite. In a recent study, the Open Society Justice Initiative defined strategic litigation as 'legal action in a court that is consciously aimed at achieving rights-related changes in law, policy, practice, and/or public awareness above and beyond relief for the named plaintiff(s)'.[78] In her recent book-length study, Helen Duffy similarly defines strategic human rights litigation (SHRL) as 'litigation that pursues goals—or which concerns interests—that are broader than only those of the immediate parties'.[79] Duffy finds that SHRL is expanding dramatically, and 'often exponentially', in both volume and 'the range of types of litigation, and the number and spread of available fora and remedies'.[80] These recent studies, as well as many others, have found that SHRL has had numerous, broad-ranging positive impacts—including direct, indirect, and even hidden impacts.[81] Studies find that SHRL can make a real difference in entrenched injustice, especially when success is measured not by a binary 'win/lose' metric, but instead by examining multidimensional impacts,

[74] Communication from B. Santosh Rao Dora, CPR-N Staff, to author (2 January 2020), on file with author.

[75] See n. 72, 8–9.

[76] Communication from B. Santosh Rao Dora (n. 74).

[77] See case study in Section 4.

[78] Open Society Justice Initiative, *Strategic Litigation Impacts: Insights from Global Experience* (2018) 25, https://www.opensocietyfoundations.org/sites/default/files/strategic-litigation-impacts-insights-20181023.pdf (last visited 12 October 2020)

[79] H. Duffy, *Strategic Human Rights Litigation: Understanding and Maximising Impact* (2018) 3.

[80] Ibid. 9.

[81] Ibid. 40.

including material, instrumental, non-material,[82] political,[83] and symbolic changes.[84] Indeed, Duffy finds that changes may occur at many different levels, including:[85]

- impacts on rights-holders,[86] including the transformation of litigants from 'victims' to activists;[87]
- impacts on law, policy, and practice;[88]
- impacts on institutions, including the strengthening of the judiciary and courts;[89]
- impacts on information and truth telling through the disclosure and dislodging of evidence and the shaping of narrative;[90]
- impacts on society and cultural change such as the shaping of issues, debates, and narratives, as well as contributions to healing and commemoration practices;[91]
- impacts on mobilization and empowerment, at the individual, community, national, and international levels;[92]
- impacts on democracy and the rule of law, including the strengthening or stabilization of the rule of law and the consolidation of democratic institutions.[93]

Duffy and others stress that impacts can be negative as well as positive—and that negative impacts can come at any of the levels outlined above.[94]

In addition to identifying and analysing these impacts, recent studies of SHRL have made a number of findings concerning litigation that align well with the legal empowerment approach. Some relevant findings relate to the significant and troubling limits and challenges inherent in the use of litigation as a human rights tool. Some of those limits are related directly to the un-democratic, sometimes elitist nature of the strategic litigation endeavour. For example, OSJI warns that lawyers should not be the only—or even the main—protagonists in strategic litigation.[95] Lawyers and activists should reinforce each other's efforts and beware not to undermine each other—something that happens all too often.[96] OSJI also found that 'a strategy of

[82] See n. 78, 18–20.

[83] A major concern, much written about in relation to strategic litigation for economic and social rights, is the impact of legalization on democratic politics. See e.g. Gauri and Brinks (n. 56) 25–28.

[84] See n. 79, 39.

[85] Ibid. 39–40.

[86] Duffy specifies a broad range of impacts on rights-holders including judicial recognition and vindication, empowerment, reparation (including compensation, restitution, rectification, cessation, protection, and access to services), accountability, investigation, and prosecution, as well as symbolic reparation in the form of apology. Ibid. 50–59.

[87] Impacts on law, policy, and practice include changes in legislation, increased enforcement, the development of national and international jurisprudence, and the shaping of remedies and procedures like *amicus curiae* interventions. Ibid. 59.

[88] Ibid. 59–63.

[89] Ibid. 67–69.

[90] Ibid. 69–72

[91] Ibid. 72–74.

[92] Ibid. 75–76.

[93] Ibid. 76–77.

[94] Ibid. 77–80.

[95] As OSJI explains, 'While litigators are required, strategic litigation is most effective when carried out principally for, and together with, non-litigators'. (n. 78) 18–20.

[96] Ibid.

filing mass or iterative cases is often more effective than seeking a single landmark judgment'.[97]

This point is one that aligns well with legal empowerment approaches, which frequently involve the filing of large numbers of legally identical cases for different individuals or communities, often by paralegals or other community justice workers instead of—or in cooperation with—lawyers. In such contexts, litigation is often seen not as the 'best' option, but as the 'least worst' option when other approaches fail. As Maru, Braima, and Jalloh explain in relation to the organization Timap for Justice in Sierra Leone:

> Timap and other legal empowerment groups treat litigation as a last resort. Courts are expensive, slow and sometimes subservient to the executive branch. Moreover, the process of litigation is so technical and removed that it's difficult to fulfill the legal empowerment ideal of placing clients in the driver's seat. Litigation can easily become 'I'll solve this for you' rather than 'we'll solve it together'.[98]

In a study of the celebrated 'Treatment Action Campaign' case in South Africa, Amy Kapczynski and Jonathan Berger conclude that this right to health case was successful in no small part because it was so closely connected to broad-based mobilization and empowerment efforts. In the late 1990s, as the HIV/AIDS epidemic raged in South Africa, the AIDS-denialist government rejected offers to make free medication available nationwide for prevention of mother-to-child-transmission (PMTCT) of HIV, deciding instead to offer the medication only at pilot sites, and even then only after a long delay. The Treatment Action Campaign (TAC)—a grassroots organization that campaigns for patients' rights in the context of the HIV epidemic—had been pushing for universal access to treatment for all those with HIV in South Africa for several years by the time it brought suit in 2001. When the government position became clear, TAC filed its case, alleging that the failure to make the medicines available across South Africa was a violation of the right to health enshrined in the constitution. TAC did not rest on its papers, though. Instead, in the time between the filing and the hearing before the High Court, TAC held workshops for its members, hosted a national treatment summit on PMTCT, and organized rallies, marches, and vigils.[99] The High Court ruled in TAC's favour, finding that the government's failure to make PMTCT medication available amounted to a violation of the right to health, and ordering the government to immediately implement a national PMTCT programme that included access to the medication. The government appealed, and TAC continued to organize. In the months before the Constitutional Court hearing on appeal, TAC held protests in numerous cities, culminating with a 5,000-person march the night preceding the hearing. On the day of the hearing, TAC members stood in line to enter wearing 'HIV-Positive' T-shirts.[100] The Court found unanimously in TAC's favour. While there is an

[97] Ibid.

[98] Maru, Braima, and Jalloh, 'Squeezing Justice Out of a Broken System: Community Paralegals in Sierra Leone', in Maru and Gauri (n. 26) 227–228.

[99] Berger and Kapczynski, 'The Story of the TAC Case: The Potential and Limits of Socio-Economic Rights Litigation in South Africa', in D. Hurwitz, M. Satterthwaite, and D. Ford (eds), *Human Rights Advocacy Stories* (2009).

[100] Ibid.

extensive literature on the significance of the *TAC* case as an historic socio-economic rights victory, Kapczynski and Berger emphasize different lessons:

> Th[e] story is less about a judgment or a doctrine than it is about a movement. More specifically, it is about the power that an organized movement can have if it makes strategic use of constitutionally entrenched and justiciable human rights, lays the groundwork necessary to give those abstract guarantees meaning, and energetically builds broad public support for its cause. TAC did the political and technical work to make the Constitutional Court's judgment seem both legally obvious and morally necessary.[101]

This moral necessity is a product not of legal reasoning but of broad mobilization built on a sense of entitlement and full civic personhood. Indeed, as Berger explained in a separate article about the case, the *TAC* case 'was not run simply as a litigation matter' but was instead run by the treatment access movement itself. This confluence of factors is not always found in strategic litigation, but it is a hallmark of how litigation is used in legal empowerment movements, and these factors can be maximized when such legal cases are grown from the grassroots up. Often, community justice workers such as paralegals or barefoot lawyers are in the perfect position to articulate claims ripe for judicial determination, identify model plaintiffs (and ensure their accountability to the broader movement), and ensure implementation of remedies following strategic wins.

From a more critical angle, another important way litigation is used in the legal empowerment context comes from the strategic use of the judicial system as a way of reinforcing rights demands from communities long excluded from (the protection of) the state. Such critical interventions are often seen as important in and of themselves, no matter the judicial outcome. As Jagganath, Phillips, and Shah explain, cases brought in Haiti against forced displacement from camps on behalf of internally displaced persons (IDPs) following the catastrophic 2010 earthquake were part of a broader mobilization strategy.[102] The strategy conceptualized lawyers as community partners and embraced the legal empowerment of IDPs through know-your-rights trainings, street demonstrations, and packing of the courtroom with rights-holders.[103] In this setting, lawyers from the Bureau des Avocats Internationaux adopted an activist approach to making the justice system accountable to the people—in ways that combined efficacy with symbolism, such as when lawyers 'responded in Haitian Creole to the judge's French to ensure that the camp representatives underst[ood] the arguments being made on their behalf'.[104] Such efforts often 'fail' formally—but they are part of what Maru, Braima, and Jalloh have described as 'squeezing justice out of a broken system',[105] and must be assessed alongside other efforts to shift power to the

[101] Ibid.

[102] Jagannath, Phillips, and Shah, 'A Right-Based Approach to Lawyering: Legal Empowerment as an Alternative to Legal Aid in Post-Disaster Haiti', 10 *Northwestern Journal of International Human Rights* (2011) 7.

[103] Ibid.

[104] Ibid. 14.

[105] See n. 98.

grassroots. As Gauri and Brinks explain when examining the judicial enforcement of social and economic rights, to benefit from human rights, those excluded 'must find some hook, some demand mechanism, to bring universal principles to bear on their own particular situation'.[106] In the climate change and environmental impact setting, strategic litigation has helped force community consultation as a procedural requirement, shifting power to the grassroots in specific moments.[107] Even when courts are not 'active and effective',[108] strategic litigation may be a way of demanding that they become more so.[109] As with movement lawyering, '[w]hen litigation is used, it is directed toward advancing specific organizing goals'.[110] In this way, rights 'are tools mobilized by social movement actors to expose injustice and pressure government officials and private actors to commit to change'.[111]

D. Accompaniment to Build Grassroots Power

While legal empowerment tools often aim to ensure that marginalized and oppressed communities can access justice through the formal legal system, other tools begin with the recognition that existing systems are shot through with injustice. In these settings, critical legal empowerment strategies such as accompaniment may be especially important, as they embody processes of bearing witness and radical observation. The Justice Power Network in the United States describes accompaniment as follows:

> Accompaniment programs promote the rights and dignity of immigrants and challenge power dynamics in immigration decision-making spaces. They provide emotional and physical solidarity to those navigating the system, and signal to the government that immigrant allies are watching. Volunteers regularly accompany immigrants or their family members to immigration court, Immigration and Customs Enforcement (ICE) check-ins, civil and criminal court, as well as to schools, hospitals, and other places. Accompaniments provide a space for volunteers and family members to journey alongside immigrants as they navigate a complicated, often terrorizing system. While Accompaniment programs differ in approach based on regional context and community needs, they help create a safe and supportive environment

[106] Gauri and Brinks (n. 56) 305.

[107] See e.g. Moodley, *Litigation to Challenge Large Extractive Projects Is Gaining Traction in Africa*, 28 June 2020, https://www.openglobalrights.org/litigation-to-challenge-extractive-projects-gaining-traction-in-africa/ (last visited 12 October 2020).

[108] Gauri and Brinks (n. 56) 305.

[109] Indeed, OSJI found that strategic litigation may be especially important in illiberal societies, where few other advocacy options exist. (n. 78).

[110] Cummings, (n. 46) 1659 (internal citations omitted) (providing the following examples of organizing goals served by litigation in movement lawyering contexts: 'supporting low-wage workers' collective demand for better pay and conditions, enabling day laborers to solicit work on street corners without reprisal, creating case-by-case precedent in individual LGBT parental rights cases that change facts on the ground in order to gradually build support for broader parenting equality goals, representing tenants in housing court as part of a campaign to resist landlords' efforts to convert affordable housing to market-rate units, and defending clients in carefully selected criminal test cases to highlight the unfair application of city zoning laws to undermine immigrant businesses').

[111] Ibid.

and often provide training and advice, supporting immigrants to best advocate for their rights.[112]

These programmes, developed by immigrant-led organizations, are designed to advance both the rights and the dignity of immigrants. Both are under direct attack in the United States: it is difficult to advance human rights in a legal system that defines many immigrants as 'illegal', and it takes acts of disobedience to reassert the dignity of individuals hauled before courts born of racialized citizenship[113] that sit in judgment of individuals' trauma.[114] Recognizing the power of simply being present and bearing witness alongside those targeted for deportation and detention, accompaniment programmes pair 'citizen-witness[es]' with individuals facing legal systems that do not recognize many of their core rights claims.[115] These accompaniers are trained to be physically present, to observe immigration authorities carefully—often noting instances of 'bureaucratic violence' such as use of ethnic slurs or derogatory language, or the refusal to provide translation—and to challenge procedural irregularities and public silence.[116] They also simply offer solidarity in the face of injustice.[117] Doing so poses an inherent challenge to the existing power dynamics inside immigration systems and upends the individualization of processes that take family members out of their homes, their communities, and their workplaces. Embodying critical praxis, for example, the New Sanctuary Coalition centres the experience of those targeted by immigration authorities, asking volunteers to refer to these community members as 'Friends' and to see themselves as allies instead of the main protagonists in efforts to transform the legal system's approach to immigration. NSC stands firm on core values that affirm that 'no person is illegal', there must be 'no deportations', that 'asylum is a human right', that the immigration enforcement agency ICE must be abolished, and that the world must embrace open borders.[118] By starting from the position that borders should be open and that immigration agencies have no recognized authority to sort people into 'authorized' and 'unauthorized' presence, the New Sanctuary Coalition rejects the legitimacy of the legal framework upon which deportations are based. Instead, NSC's grounding is in a moral commitment to 'creating sanctuary anywhere our Friends feel threatened'.[119]

Using similar methods but based in Austin, Texas, Grassroots Leadership uses the strategy of accompaniment in both the immigration and the criminal justice system

[112] Justice Power Network, *Accompaniment*, https://justicepower.org/accompaniment/ (last visited 12 October 2020).

[113] For a discussion of the racialization of citizenship, see Fitzgerald, 'The History of Racialized Citizenship', in A. Shachar *et al.* (eds), *The Oxford Handbook of Citizenship* (2017).

[114] As the Justice Power Network website explains, 'The U.S. immigration system is hostile; it turns human beings into "A numbers", considers their existence to be illegal, and requires them to relive past trauma in order to fit within a narrow legal category.' (n. 112).

[115] New Sanctuary Coalition, *What We Do*, https://www.newsanctuarynyc.org/what_we_do (last visited 12 October 2020). It should be noted that some organizations encourage non-citizens as well as citizens to engage in accompaniment.

[116] See n. 112.

[117] Ibid.

[118] New Sanctuary Coalition, *Core Values*, https://www.newsanctuarynyc.org/who_is_nsc (last visited 12 October 2020).

[119] n. 115.

to address the impacts of '*crimmigration*'—the 'unique or uniquely harsh methods of regulating the lives of migrants' in the United States.[120] Through a programme called 'Court Watch', volunteers—many of whom are themselves non-citizens—show up in spaces where immigrants are criminalized and othered, documenting all forms of discrimination, procedural irregularity, and injustice—from ubiquitous forms of unfairness such as excessive wait times, to overt instances of exclusion like the criminalization of border crossing. Such witnessing is aimed at 'hold[ing] judges and attorneys accountable'.[121]

The work of these accompaniment programmes is hard to quantify but profound: as the Justice Power Network explains, 'it is likely that eyes on the system lead to reduced bond fees, grants of parole, decisions not to detain an individual, and even avert deportations'.[122] It also turns witnesses into allies who find their place alongside those directly impacted, who are leading movements to transform the immigration system.[123] In this way accompaniment is a tool of critical legal empowerment, building the power of such movements to demand thoroughgoing change in a system thoroughly shaped by the injustice of racialized citizenship and criminalized human presence.

4. Case Study: Redefining Access to Justice through Legal Empowerment of Indigenous Communities in Guyana

If legal empowerment has significant contributions to make to human rights advocacy in this moment of crisis, those contributions may be especially apparent in relation to communities that are facing some of the forces seen as most troublesome for the rights project today. The use of legal empowerment approaches by Indigenous Peoples and their communities that sit on the frontlines of climate change, face intense pressure to integrate into neoliberal capitalism from national governments and NGOs, as well as inter- and non-governmental international actors, and articulate rights claims that often exceed the bounds of existing interpretations of formal law, provide an opportunity to assess whether legal empowerment approaches can help recalibrate the human rights endeavour. This section will examine the work of the South Rupununi District Council in Guyana (SRDC),[124] suggesting that SRDC's deployment of legal empowerment approaches—and its partnerships with external allies supporting these strategies—has allowed it to stand up to these forces in ways that can teach us useful lessons for human rights.

[120] See Hernández, *Defining Crimmigration Law: Part I*, http://crimmigration.com/2015/09/17/defining-crimmigration-law-part-1/ (last visited 12 October 2020).

[121] See n. 112.

[122] Ibid.

[123] Ibid.

[124] This case study was reviewed and approved for publication by the SRDC. The work examined here has been undertaken by SRDC (and its partner NGO and secretariat, the South Central Peoples Development Association (SCPDA)) with the support of several allies, including the Guyana-based Amerindian Peoples Association and the National Toshaos Council, as well as international allies including, inter alia, Forest Peoples' Programme, Digital Democracy, Rainforest Foundation USA, the World Wildlife Fund, and the Global Justice Clinic at NYU School of Law (which the author directs).

The SRDC, a collective governance body of the indigenous Wapichan community of the Southern Rupununi in Guyana, is using numerous approaches that fit within the rubric of legal empowerment to advance their human rights to self-determination and equality. Through enunciation of customary law through their own institutions, participatory mapping, community monitoring, and advocacy with government institutions, the SRDC has been expanding its ability to exercise self-determination as Indigenous Peoples while making specific claims as equal citizens of the state of Guyana. To advance its rights, the community has used all three of the 'know, use, and shape law' elements of legal empowerment, also advancing critical legal empowerment claims for transformation, though it does not often use these terms. Through an examination of SRDC's experience, this brief case study aims to demonstrate how critical legal empowerment can enhance the agency of rights-holders in ways that traditional human rights advocacy might not.[125]

A. Know Law: Enunciation of Customary Law; Engagement with National and International Law

'Knowing' law in this indigenous[126] context, as in many others, involves not only knowing the national and international law protecting the rights of Indigenous Peoples, but also—most importantly, and as an antecedent to knowledge of these exogenous systems of law—knowing and affirming the customary law of the community itself. In the early 2000s, the Wapichan community of the South Rupununi undertook an intensive, participatory research project to identify and articulate customary norms. This effort spanned several years and culminated in a report entitled *Wa Wiizi, Wa Kaduzu/Our Territory, Our Custom.*[127] The report sets out customary norms concerning Wapichan *wiizi* (territory) and the use of biological resources within Wapichan *wiizi*. Crucially, the process used to identify and document these norms was intensively collaborative, involving 'visits to 17 major settlements, visits to many minor settlements, 257 separate interviews with elders, leaders and community members, 17 public meetings, and over 30 site visits to different resource areas'.[128] Mainstream human rights methods for protecting the land rights of Indigenous Peoples often begins by identifying national and international laws that support land claims without attending to the relevant customary law. This approach decentres the

[125] The information in this case study is drawn from publicly available materials and does not include privileged or confidential information.

[126] I capitalize the 'I' in Indigenous as a sign of respect and equality (e.g. 'Indigenous' is an identity, capitalized alongside others such as 'French' or 'Spanish'), and to make clear that it is a noun, differentiating from the adjective 'indigenous'.

[127] B. David *et al.*, *Wa Wiizi—Wa Kaduzu/Our Territory—Our Custom: Customary Use of Biological Resources and Related Traditional Practices within Wapichan Territory in Guyana* (Abridged Version 1.3, 2006), http://wapichanao.communitylands.org/1499798142646-wa_wiizi_wa_kaduzu.pdf (last visited 12 October 2020).

[128] Ibid. 8 (further explaining that 'In accordance with customary methods of investigation, the researchers engaged in informal discussions ("gaffing") with holders of traditional knowledge in the early morning, in the evenings or after *manoru* work (collective self-help), often over a traditional gourd of *parakari* (cassava beer)', as well as desk research).

community's most important knowledge and can have a profoundly disempowering impact. Legal empowerment necessarily begins with the community's own sense of entitlement—its own conception of its rights—and its own legal system. Beginning here is especially important in indigenous contexts, since indigenous communities have borne the brunt of epistemic violence for generations. 'Knowing' customary law involves honouring forms of law that may have been hidden, silenced, and even violently repressed by colonial systems. For the Wapichan of the Southern Rupununi, using a methodology that relied on the knowledge of elders, leaders, and the broader community allowed the community to centre customary law concerning territory and biological resources before looking to exogenous sources of law that could be enlisted to support the community's claims. As Daniel Brinks has written, the process of recording the customary law of Indigenous Peoples must not essentialize those systems, lest the living nature of norms be transformed and made overly static.[129] The inclusion of the broader community in efforts to identify and formulate customary law is one way to ensure that this process enhances the legal agency of the community 'in the production and reproduction of norms'.[130]

For the Wapichan of the Southern Rupununi, the written formulation of customary law has been iterative and purpose-driven.[131] The enunciation of norms concerning territorial management, biological resource conservation, and use of natural resources has been prioritized, since these have been most relevant to the community's most pressing legal concerns: confirmation of title over Wapichan *wiizi*, protection of the resources within the Wapichan *wiizi*, and regulation of the activities of outsiders on this traditional territory.[132] As explained in *Wa Wiizi, Wa Kaduzu*, the sustainable use of land and resources by the Wapichan depends on the 'maintenance of the customary land tenure regime', which is 'threatened by inadequate land titles that do not recognize the extensive pattern of customary occupation and use'.[133] Thus, for the Wapichan of the Southern Rupununi, *knowing* customary law in turn demands that the community know, use, and shape—or transform—domestic and international law in order to advance the aims of the Wapichan people.

Indeed, 'knowing' customary law is crucial in part because international and domestic law concerning Indigenous Peoples involves comprehending systems of law that have been intensely oppressive from their inception. Distinctions between the 'civilized' and the 'barbaric' are fundamental to international law, and colonialist legal–political ideologies including the 'discovery' doctrine and the doctrine of *terra nullius* have been used to justify genocide, dispossession, and forced assimilation from the time of first contact well into the modern era.[134] Thus, Indigenous Peoples necessarily

[129] Brinks, 'Access to What? Legal Agency and Access to Justice for Indigenous Peoples in Latin America', 55 *Journal of Development Studies* (2019) 348, at 356. Indeed, this kind of stasis has been a legacy of colonialism in many places.

[130] Ibid.

[131] n. 127, 5 (noting that the study was undertaken using a community-inclusive, collaborative manner with the goal of 'seek[ing] respect for our customary land rights and effective protection for all the cultural and biological diversity in our homeland').

[132] Ibid. 3–5.

[133] Ibid. 4.

[134] See generally S. Anaya, *Indigenous Peoples in International Law* (2009) 37–53. As Jessie Hohmann explains, 'From the earliest encounters of Westphalian international law and Indigenous peoples, international law operated so as to bring Indigenous peoples within its reach, yet deny them the benefits of its

come to any encounter with formal law with a finely tuned sense of how the law has been used to *disempower*. This perspective engenders a well-founded critical consciousness that serves communities well when they begin to work intensively with national and international law. At that point, communities approach legal empowerment by asking when and how national and international law can be used to advance their agency and self-determination, and when the law is ill-suited to such goals, requiring transformation. The answer will be highly context-specific, given the broadly varying circumstances for the rights of Indigenous Peoples under national legal systems. At the international level, however, thanks to several decades of advocacy by Indigenous Peoples, international human rights law now includes robust norms recognizing the rights of Indigenous Peoples to self-determination, equality, and full participation and consent to development initiatives.[135]

'Knowing' national and international law for the Wapichan of the Southern Rupununi means knowing how the law has been both empowering and disempowering. The central example is the way that the state of Guyana has both accepted and rejected claims by the Wapichan people for title of Wapichan *wiizi*. At the time of Guyana's independence from the United Kingdom, the new state undertook to recognize 'the legal ownership of lands, rights of occupancy and other legal rights held by custom or tradition' by the Indigenous Peoples of Guyana as a condition of its very independence.[136] The Guyana Amerindian Lands Commission (ALC) was set up in 1966 to fulfil this agreement.[137] Wapichan communities in the Southern Rupununi presented claims for communal title in the areas encompassing Wapichan *wiizi*.[138] The Commissioners rejected these claims, finding the land claim to have been 'excessive and beyond the ability of the residents to successfully administrate and develop'.[139] Instead of full title, only 11 of the 22 principal communities received any title—and even these titles do not include the full claim for the relevant areas, leaving many families outside the titled land. However:

> [o]ur communities have never accepted this assertion made by the ALC. We maintain that we do indeed have capacity to administer our territory and the Wapichan people have an inherent right to own and control the full extent of our traditional lands … We continue to demand that legal title be given to the communities over their land.[140]

Knowing the legal standards that have been used to refuse full land rights, the Wapichan communities of the South Rupununi have engaged in numerous processes

protection'. 'Chapter 6: The UNDRIP and the Rights of Indigenous Peoples to Existence, Cultural Integrity and Identity, and Non-Assimilation: Articles 7(2), 8, and 43', in J. Hohmann and M. Weller (eds), *The UN Declaration on the Rights of Indigenous Peoples: A Commentary* (2018) 152.

135 See n. 134, 55–132.
136 n. 127, at 12.
137 Ibid. 13.
138 Ibid.
139 Ibid. (quoting Amerindian Lands Commission).
140 Ibid.

aimed at demonstrating their continuous 'ability' to 'administer' Wapichan *wiizi*. As discussed above, the description of customary norms concerning land and natural resource use has been a crucial element in this effort. Further, by knowing their rights under the Amerindian Act—the framework law for the rights of Indigenous Peoples in Guyana—the SRDC was able to obtain recognition as the first self-governing representative body, or District Council, by the government of Guyana.[141] In tandem, the SRDC has entered into official land talks with the government of Guyana, regulated by an agreed Terms of Reference.[142]

B. Use Law: Participatory Mapping and Community Monitoring

As mentioned above, and like many Indigenous Peoples, the SRDC has been granted title to only some portions of its customary lands:

> Our foreparents began work for the full recognition of our territory in the nineteenth century, yet only pieces of our land were recognised in the 1930s. In 1967 a group of our leaders came together to present a written request for legal title to all of our lands in Wapichan wiizi in submissions and letters presented to the Amerindian Lands Commission. Some further land titles were received in 1991, but still did not cover the full extent of our lands.[143]

Therefore, a constant priority has been seeking government recognition for the extension of those titled areas to encompass the remainder of the traditional Wapichan territory in the Southern Rupununi. While 'those in power have employed maps over the centuries to mark off and control territories inhabited by indigenous peoples', recent decades have seen the emergence of mapping by Indigenous Peoples with the aim of defending land rights.[144] For the Wapichan of the Southern Rupununi, participatory mapping—in which the community itself worked to map its 'traditional occupation and use of land', through traditional names, places, and practices in a way that made those forms of knowledge legible to both the community and the official eye—began in 2000, and has always been aimed at, inter alia, gaining legal recognition of the entirety of Wapichan *wiizi*.[145] These activities have resulted in what might be

[141] Filippo del Gatto/Rainforest Foundation USA, *Protecting Forests through Protecting Rights in Guyana* (June 2018) 17, https://rainforestfoundation.org/wp-content/uploads/2018/08/Protecting-Forests-Through-Protecting-Rights-in-Guyana.pdf (last visited 12 October 2020). The Amerindian Act of 2006 provides for the creation of District Councils as representative indigenous organizations. See Amerindian Act 2006, ss. 35–36.

[142] RFUS (n. 141) 9–10.

[143] South Central and South Rupununi Districts Toshaos Councils, *Baokopa'o wa di'itinpan wadaun nii nao ati: Kaimanamana'o, wa zaamatapan, wa di'itapan na'apamnii wa sha'apatan Wapichan wiizi Guyana'ao raza/Thinking Together for Those Coming Behind Us: An Outline Plan for the Care of Wapichan Territory in Guyana* (2012) iv, https://www.forestpeoples.org/sites/fpp/files/publication/2012/05/wapichan-mp-22may12lowresnomarks.pdf (last visited 12 October 2020).

[144] For an overview of the field of Indigenous mapping, see Chapin, Lamb, and Threlkeld, 'Mapping Indigenous Lands', *Annual Review of Anthropology* (2005) 619, at 620.

[145] South Central and South Rupununi Districts Toshaos Councils (n. 143) iv.

called 'living maps'[146] that are continually updated so that more than 4,750km^2 of land is now represented with toponymic accuracy. As Fred Pearce explained in 2015:

> [T]o justify their claim the [Wapichan of the Southern Rupununi] have mapped and catalogued their territory in far greater detail, and with much more accuracy, even than the government. The main maps are now done—with 40,000 digital points collated... and detailed notes from interviews with elders about the importance of every creek, homestead and forest clearing. And they have developed a plan to protect it, using traditional knowledge and methods of land use—in particular through the creation of a large community forest, managed and protected for hunting and gathering, for swidden farming and for science and tourism.[147]

Of crucial importance is the fact that some of the information collected by the Wapichan mappers is sensitive and thus not included on published versions of the maps. This information, concerning settlements with graves and the locations of spiritual sites, is protected by the community and not shared with outsiders.[148]

Further, in an act of continuous custodial relation to Wapichan *wiizi*, the Wapichan of the Southern Rupununi have used these community-generated maps as the basis of a monitoring programme aimed at curbing 'external developments in *Wapichan wiizi* and the growing pressures coming from mining, logging, roads and other activities'.[149] Not only do the maps serve as a base layer for information about unlawful activities gathered by community monitors, they are also updated in real time through the mapping work of the monitors. In these ways, the monitoring programme is a living method for using the law to advance the self-determination rights of the Wapichan.

Community monitors are selected by their villages and receive training in data collection using smartphones, operation of drones built and operated by the SRDC, and they report to Village Councils and the District Council.[150] Focusing on extractive activities, the SRDC's monitors map and gather data concerning gold mining, logging, fishing, cattle rustling, and other activities carried out without the permission of the local villages or the SRDC.[151] While most—if not all—of these activities are unlawful under Wapichan customary law, in recent years, the SRDC has turned its attention to using the laws of Guyana and international law to bolster its claims concerning these impermissible activities. Monitors are now being trained in the legal provisions relevant to the data they collect, including those drawn from, inter alia, Guyanese law concerning mining, forestry, the environment, and the rights of Amerindian communities.

146 Thanks to Fergus MacKay for this term; personal communication with author, 2 July 2020.

147 Fred Pearce/Forest Peoples Programme, *Where They Stand* (2015) 6, https://www.forestpeoples.org/sites/fpp/files/publication/2015/10/where-they-standweb-spreads.pdf (last visited 12 October 2020).

148 Ibid. 13.

149 South Central and South Rupununi Districts Toshaos Councils (n. 143) iv.

150 South Rupununi District Council, 'Executive Summary', *Wapichan Environmental Monitoring Report*, September 2018 (hereinafter SRDC, *Wapichan Environmental Monitoring Report*), http://wapichanao.com munitylands.org/1548691773093-wapichan-environmental-monitoring-report-2018-v2.pdf (last visited 12 October 2020).

151 Ibid.

In autumn 2018, the SRDC published its first environmental monitoring report, presenting data on dozens of instances of mining unlawful under Guyanese and customary law, including the following:

- Between 2013–18, our monitors have made more than 250 observations of activities that are harmful, illegal, and/or violations of our rights.
- Between 2013–18, our monitors have observed more than 380 impacts on the environment and our way of life, including deforestation, water pollution, destruction of hunting and fishing grounds, and damage to cultural heritage, among others.
- Almost 50 per cent of the impacts observed by monitors are caused by mining activities.[152]

The report showed that mining activity has been concentrated on Marutu Taawa (known as Marudi Mountain in English), where Guyana Goldstrike, a Canadian company, holds a permit to move forward with large-scale gold mining.[153] This mountain lies within traditional Wapichan territory.[154] As the company seeks investments sufficient to advance these plans, it allows small-scale miners to work within its concession, where they have been documented using mercury in processing gold.[155] A study published in 2020 found that 100 per cent of adult residents sampled in a nearby SRDC village had hair mercury levels exceeding WHO standards as a result of eating mercury-contaminated fish.[156] The SRDC had not provided free, prior, and informed consent for these activities on Marutu Taawa, 'an important spiritual, cultural, and resource-gathering site' for the Wapichan of the South Rupununi.[157] On this basis (among others), the SRDC called for the rejection of Guyana Goldstrike's recently submitted environmental and social impact assessment (ESIA).[158]

In September 2018, the SRDC presented its environmental report to the head of government, President David Granger, calling on him to officially recognize and collaborate with the SRDC's monitoring programme and to reject Guyana Goldstrike's ESIA.[159] In response, the President promised not to 'sweep the problems under the carpet', and said he would create a multi-agency task force to respond to the SRDC's environmental concerns.[160]

[152] Ibid.

[153] Ibid. 13.

[154] Ibid. 13.

[155] Ibid. 13, 15, 18, 22, 25.

[156] Watson *et al.*, 'Survey of Methylmercury Exposures and Risk Factors Among Indigenous Communities in Guyana, South America', 10 *Journal of Health & Pollution* 1 (2020).

[157] SRDC, *Wapichan Environmental Monitoring Report*, 150, i.

[158] Ibid. 27–28; see also Stabroek News, *South Rupununi Council Objects to Romanex's Proposed Marudi Mountain Mine-Claims Lack of Consultation for Impact Assessment* (30 Sept. 2018), https://www.stabroeknews.com/2018/09/30/news/guyana/south-rupununi-council-objects-to-romanexs-proposed-marudi-mountain-mine/ (last visited 12 October 2020).

[159] SRDC, *Indigenous Council's First Environmental Monitoring Report Prompts Presidential Action in Guyana—SRDC Calls for Government Recognition and Collaboration to Combat Treats Posed by Mining in Wapichan Territory*, 20 November 2018, https://chrgj.org/wp-content/uploads/2018/11/SRDC-Monitoring-Report-Announcement-Final-11.20.2018.pdf (last visited 12 October 2020).

[160] Department of Public Information (Guyana), *President Granger Orders Multi-Agency Task Force to Tackle South Rupununi Problems*, 17 September 2018, https://dpi.gov.gy/president-granger-orders-multi-agency-task-force-to-tackle-south-rupununi-problems/ (last visited 12 October 2020).

Pressing forward to monitor the full effects of extractive activities on Wapichan *wiizi*, in 2019, the SRDC added a scientific element to its monitoring programme. Community monitors are now trained to conduct field measurements to check for impacts of extractive activities on water quality within Wapichan *wiizi*.[161] These field measurements are then compared with national and international benchmarks and regulations concerning safe water. As SRDC has explained, these scientific measurements are intended to supplement—not displace—traditional ways of knowing about the environment. As one SRDC monitor explained:

> We know about the importance of protecting our lands and our waters because this is impressed upon us by our fore-parents. I have also learned about the environment through interactions with indigenous communities and because of my connection to nature itself. This means that for a long time, I've been able to look at water and know from my observations and experience whether it is contaminated. However, learning about scientific principles allows me to explain changes in water quality that I have long observed but never been able to explain in scientific terms.[162]

This kind of explanation is important as the SRDC pursues government action to remedy water damage, stop unlawful mining, and extend title to Wapichan *wiizi*. As this monitor explained, the combination of scientific data and knowledge of the law can be powerful:

> Learning about the international and Guyanese laws that protect our rights strengthens our ability to use this data as information to influence both the miners who are causing harm, and also the government authorities and decision makers who have an obligation to regulate mining and protect our environment, but are presently falling short of their responsibilities.[163]

The SRDC mapping and monitoring programme thus plays multiple roles: it asserts the community's protective and custodial gaze across all of *Wapichan wiizi*; it documents activities it labels as unlawful in real time; and it provides evidence of activities that amount to unlawful acts under customary law and may amount to violations of the law of Guyana and international law. In all of these ways, the SRDC is 'using' law as a tool of empowerment through its monitoring programme. In fact, the empowerment the SRDC is enacting here can be seen as a form of 'performative ontology' as articulated by TWAIL scholar Jayson Lamchek.[164] By using customary law alongside formal, state-recognized law, and by using it in *all* of Wapichan *wiizi*—not only the formally titled areas—the SRDC is enacting a form of resistance that 'breathes life into' rights.[165]

[161] SRDC, *SRDC Launches Water Monitoring Pilot to Protect the Wapichanao Right to Water: The Global Justice Clinic and Water Scientist Lend Support to Crucial New Effort*, March 2019, http://wapichanao.com munitylands.org/news.html (last visited 12 October 2020).

[162] Ibid.

[163] Ibid.

[164] Lamchek, 'Exercising Rights into Existence: New Human Rights Strategies by Third World Peoples', 19 *Australian Journal of Human Rights* (2013) 175.

[165] Fergus MacKay, personal communication with author, 2 July 2020.

C. Shape and Transform Law: Law and Policy Reform Efforts

The Wapichan of the Southern Rupununi have long engaged in efforts to *shape* the law—to reform, amend, and extend the protections of the laws of Guyana. From the time of external contact, legal norms have been used to dispossess Wapichan communities. In the face of these violations, the Wapichan have sought legal recognition of their land claims—first from colonial powers and later from the modern state of Guyana. For example, in the nineteenth century, when Wapichan were made vulnerable to slave raiders from Brazil, they sought both assistance in defending themselves from the raiders and recognition of their land claims from the colonial government in Georgetown.[166] They were successful in obtaining protection, but instead of granting title, their land was declared to be 'Crown lands', where colonists succeeded in obtaining grazing rights.[167] Similar conditions prevailed until the time of Guyana's independence, when—as described above—the Wapichan presented their land claim to the Guyana Amerindian Lands Commission; efforts to obtain the relevant titles continue to this day.[168]

While the Wapichan have engaged with the prevailing legal systems to seek their rights, they have also continuously engaged in efforts to change the laws that have disempowered and disadvantaged them. As explained in *Wa Wiizi, Wa Kaduzu/Our Territory, Our Custom*, Guyanese law has 'included measures intended to protect the traditional rights of indigenous peoples',[169] such as the Constitution's Article 149G, which states that 'Indigenous peoples shall have the right to the protection, preservation and promulgation of their languages, cultural heritage and way of life'.[170] However, provisions like this, dating as far back as the early nineteenth century[171] 'have not always been upheld in practice and have been systematically contracted over the centuries'.[172] In recent years, the Wapichan communities of the Southern Rupununi have repeatedly called for reform and revision of the 2006 Amerindian Act, which 'provide[s] only very limited protections for customary natural resource management systems', fails 'to adequately recognise indigenous systems of governance and jurisdiction', and does not 'recognise customary land and resource ownership rights in protected areas', among other shortcomings.[173] For these reasons, the SRDC's engagement in efforts to shape the law include the transformative call for greater recognition of the Council's governance space through 'ownership and control' of Wapichan *wiizi*.[174] As Daniel Brinks has written of legal empowerment efforts by Indigenous Peoples:

166 n. 127, 11–13.
167 Ibid.
168 Ibid.
169 Ibid. 53.
170 Constitution of Guyana, Art. 149G.
171 Fergus MacKay, personal communication with author, 2 July 2020.
172 n. 127, 53.
173 Ibid. 55–56.
174 Ibid.

> the goal is not to secure the same substantive notions of justice [as in the ambient community], but rather to pursue alternative ones altogether, ones that will more closely reflect their own [indigenous] normative framework. For indigenous groups and other communities bound by a common identity, this means not only finding ways to enhance agency within the formal system, but also expanding the reach of customary, indigenous legal systems.[175]

To strengthen their calls for transformation, the SRDC has partnered with national and international organizations to amplify the demand for revision of the Amerindian Act.[176] This successful effort has led to recommendations from the UN Committee on the Elimination of Racial Discrimination and the UN Committee on the Elimination of All Forms of Discrimination Against Women to the government of Guyana seeking revision of the Amerindian Act to ensure the full range of rights guaranteed to the Wapichan as Indigenous Peoples are protected under formal law in Guyana.[177] In addition to advocating for revision of the broad national framework law for Indigenous Peoples, the SRDC has called for revision and reform of a variety of other legal provisions and policies that impact their rights and interests. These efforts have drawn on Wapichan customary law concerning resource use, and they encompass calls for reform of Guyana's Wildlife Regulations,[178] the laws and regulations concerning environmental impact assessments,[179] and numerous policies concerning resource use.[180]

The SRDC's engagement in law and policy advocacy can be seen as an example of what Rodríguez-Garavito and Arenas describe as a process of 'legal innovation' led by Indigenous Peoples:

175 See n. 129.

176 The Wapichan of the Southern Rupununi (represented by the SRDC, Village councils, and their partner NGO SCPDA have, over the years, partnered with numerous national and international organizations, including, inter alia, the Amerindian Peoples' Association; Digital Democracy, the Forest Peoples' Programme, the Global Justice Clinic at NYU School of Law; Rainforest Foundation USA; and Size of Wales.

177 See e.g. UN Committee on the Elimination of Racial Discrimination, Consideration of reports submitted by States Parties under article 9 of the Convention—Concluding observations of the Committee on the Elimination of Racial Discrimination: Guyana, UN Doc. CERD/C/GUY/CO/14 (2006) ('The Committee urges the State party to remove the discriminatory distinction between titled and untitled communities from the 2006 Amerindian Act and from any other legislation ... the Committee is deeply concerned about the lack of legal recognition of the rights of ownership and possession of indigenous communities over the lands which they traditionally occupy and about the State party's practice of granting land titles excluding bodies of waters and subsoil resources to indigenous communities on the basis of numerical and other criteria not necessarily in accordance with the traditions of indigenous communities concerned, thereby depriving untitled and ineligible communities of rights to lands they traditionally occupy'); UN Committee on Economic, Social and Cultural Rights, *Concluding Observations on the Combined Second to Fourth Periodic Reports of Guyana*, United Nations Economic and Social Council, UN Doc. E/C.12/GUY/CO/2-4, para. 15 (28 Oct. 2015) (finding that the lack of legal recognition and ownership over Wapichan *wiizi* to be a violation of the rights of the Wapichan as an Indigenous People); UN Committee on the Elimination of Discrimination Against Women, *Concluding Observations on the Ninth Periodic Report of Guyana*, UN Doc. CEDAW/C/GUY/CO/9 (2019) (calling on the government of Guyana to 'Amend the Amerindian Act (2006) and other relevant laws, using a gender-sensitive approach, with a view to ensuring that the rights of Amerindian communities to their lands, territories and resources are fully recognized and protected, in accordance with the United Nations Declaration on the Rights of Indigenous Peoples').

178 n. 127, 57.

179 Ibid. 58.

180 Ibid. 57–58.

> the transnational mobilization of indigenous peoples has unleashed a process of legal innovation with profound implications for national constitutional systems and the international human rights regime. Centered on the recognition of collective rights and embodied by myriad constitutional reforms and new international legal instruments, this 'renaissance of indigenous peoples for the law' has shaken the individualist and Western-centric tenets of liberal legal thought and institutions and holds out the prospect for a cosmopolitan reconstruction of human rights.[181]

Indeed, this substantive renaissance, when coupled with a critical legal empowerment approach, holds many lessons for human rights advocacy. By centring the visions, experience, and agency of those whose rights have been systematically violated, the use of critical legal empowerment by Indigenous Peoples can model a shift that could be applied more broadly to human rights efforts in many places around the world. Professional human rights advocates and lawyers would do well to ask whether their work is led by those most affected by injustice, whether they are directly accountable to rights-holders, and whether strategies like strategic litigation and law reform, which require engagement with lawyers and legal systems, are pursued in ways that effectively shift power to those whose rights are at stake.

5. Conclusion: Critical Legal Empowerment's Lessons for Human Rights

What lessons might a focus on critical legal empowerment bring to human rights in its current moment of crisis? It could be persuasively argued that most (if not all) of what legal empowerment offers is already present within human rights practice—at least good, accountable, human rights (if not Human Rights) practice. This is in many ways true—some forms of human rights advocacy, especially those that are explicitly rights-based, movement-centred, decolonial, or community-accountable—are aimed at capacitating rights-holders and reshaping the state and other powerful institutions from the bottom up. What a focus on critical legal empowerment offers, however, is something that can be forgotten or distorted when human rights advocacy is tethered more to norms and standards and less to the realities of rights-holders' daily struggles: a commitment to transformative leadership by the grassroots. In this way, such efforts to know, use, shape—and transform—the law to reflect communities' own visions of justice form part of 'an unprecedented effervescence of debate and experimentation in bottom-up legal reform and new international legal regimes'.[182] By decentring human rights advocates and recentring leadership in the grassroots, the critical legal empowerment endeavour insists that any such experimentation be carried out by and for those with most at stake. Ultimately, critical legal empowerment is about the transformation of power relations that result when the disempowered and

[181] Rodríguez-Garavito and Arenas, 'Indigenous Rights, Transnational Activism, and Legal Mobilization: The Struggle of the U-Wa People in Colombia', in de Sousa Santos and Rodríguez-Garavito (n. 17) 243 (internal citations omitted).

[182] De Sousa Santos and Rodríguez-Garavito (n. 17) 2.

excluded make claims through—and of—legal systems that have been designed to oppress them. Such a transformation may be implicit in human rights norms, but in recent decades, human rights has been seen to be either unable or unwilling to respond to rapidly increasing inequality, the systemic race-based oppression, climate change, and the rise of surveillance capitalism. The commitment to building the power of grassroots leadership makes clear that rights are always political; they demand engagement especially with the most persistent forms of inequality and injustice; and they insist that engagement cannot be 'in the name of' communities whose own voices must define the path forward.

Index

For the benefit of digital users, indexed terms that span two pages (e.g., 52–53) may, on occasion, appear on only one of those pages.